For hundreds of years ___ drunk only in Scotland. ___ spirit drink, accounts fo ___ export earnings, and is available in every ___. Yet one aspect of this extraordinary drink will never change. It can only be made in Scotland.

The secrets of the unique ingredients and distilling processes are just a few of the mysteries that Richard Grindal unravels in *The Spirit of Whisky*. In an entertaining tour of the Highlands, Lowlands and islands of Scotland he discusses every aspect of the making and partaking of Scotch, following its evolution from the 'acquavitae' first recorded in 1494 to the present-day amber nectar. He reveals that for centuries malt whisky was the traditional drink of the Scots. Today with more than a hundred distilleries, each with a history often stretching back to the days of illicit stills and whisky smugglers and each making a 'single' whisky with a distinctive flavour and character of its own, malt whisky still reigns supreme. Yet it was the blending process, developed amidst bitter controversy by the 'Whisky Barons' – the Dewars, Buchanans, Walkers and Haigs – that brought Scotch to international attention.

In a narrative spiced with anecdotes from his twenty years in the trade, Richard Grindal introduces us to noble malts ranging from Talisker to the much mis-pronounced Glenmorangie (think of 'orange' and you've got it right) and offers his selection and that of experts of the twelve finest. We meet many of the characters – past and present – who form the legend of the world's most famous drink. Offering tips on how to select and enjoy whisky, and discussing the controversial subject of how to drink it, Richard Grindal provides the reassuring advice that there is only one way to do so and that is the way you enjoy it.

'If a body could just find oot the
exac' proper proportion and quantity that ought
to be drunk every day, and keep to that, I verily trow that
he might leeve for ever, without dying at a', and that
doctors and kirkyards would go oot o' fashion.'

James Hogg – *The Ettrick Shepherd*

THE SPIRIT OF WHISKY

AN AFFECTIONATE ACCOUNT OF THE WATER OF LIFE

RICHARD GRINDAL

WARNER BOOKS

A Warner Book

First published in Great Britain in 1992 by Warner Books

Copyright © 1992 by Richard Grindal

The right of Richard Grindal to be identified as
author of this work has been asserted by
him in accordance with the Copyright, Designs
and Patents Act 1988.

A CIP catalogue record for this book is available from the British Library

ISBN 0 7474 10402

Typeset by Leaper & Gard Ltd, Bristol, England
Printed and bound in Great Britain by
Cox & Wyman Ltd, Reading

Warner Books
A Division of
Little, Brown and Company (UK) Limited
165 Great Dover Street
London SE1 4YA

Contents

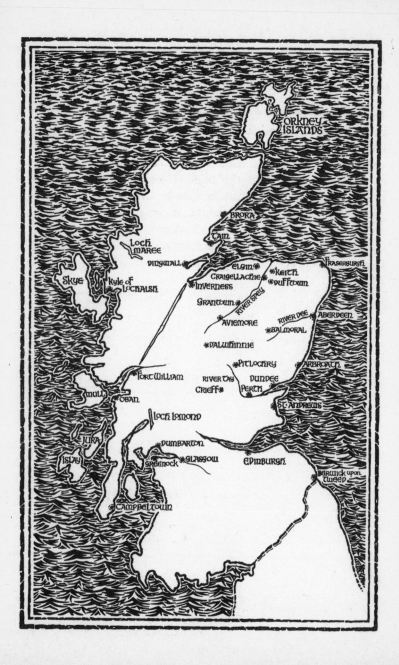

Acknowledgements

So many of my friends in the whisky business have given me encouragement and advice in the writing of this book that it would be impractical to name them all and in any case many of them are named in the book. I feel I must, however, express my special thanks to Trevor Cowan and Richard Paterson, both among Scotland's leading whisky blenders, and to my colleagues in the Scotch Whisky Association, Quintin Stewart, Tony Tucker, Yvonne Scott and Campbell Evans for their practical and willing help.

1

The Beginning

We had met by chance in the City Lights Bar, 107 floors above Manhattan in the World Trade Center. Chester was an octogenarian, remarkably alert, with one of those small Ronald Colman moustaches which were coming back into fashion and wearing what Americans at that time seemed to believe the British always wore, a Harris tweed sports jacket and grey worsted slacks. We were both drinking Scotch, which is always introduction enough, and slipped easily into conversation. When I asked if he were married, he told me that he had been married twice, but that sadly both his wives had, as he put it, shuffled off this mortal coil.

'My first wife died during Prohibition,' he added, 'through drinking yack yack bourbon.'

I had read enough about Prohibition to know that yack yack bourbon, together with jackass brandy, happy sally and soda pop moon, was one of the many drinks produced during the long dry years in illicit alky stills in American cities and sold in speakeasies. Some were made with industrial alcohol and could be lethal.

'I pushed my second wife off the top of the Empire State Building,' Chester went on reflectively, as though he were still savouring the moment.

'Good God! Why?'

'She didn't like bourbon.'

His face was stern but his eyes were smiling, which told me he must have Celtic blood. They also told me he was having a sly joke at a gullible Scot's expense. I learned then that his wife – his only wife – was alive and that they had been happily married for more than sixty years.

Chester was keen to talk about Scotch, for although he had drunk it for as long as he could recall, his knowledge, especially of single malt Scotches, was limited. It seemed to me that I could learn from him too. Here was a man, the course of whose life ran almost parallel with the years that had seen the remarkable rise of Scotch Whisky to pre-eminence among the drinks of the world. Admittedly whisky was being shipped overseas from Scotland before Prohibition began, but the amounts exported were relatively small and those who drank it were in the main expatriate Scots or Englishmen who had settled in the colonies and dominions of the British Empire. I knew of course how, over the past eighty years, Scotch had achieved its international reputation and the events which had led to its finding a place in the bars and restaurants and homes of more than two hundred countries.

What interested me was why. Why is it, I have often
wondered, that the national drink of a tiny country has been
so readily accepted by people of totally different cultures,
social customs and gastronomic tastes? Why was it that in a
New York bar Chester and I were able that evening to choose
from a selection of more than a hundred and twenty-five
different Scotches, a selection that not more than half a dozen
bars in Scotland could match?

Many Scots take the success of Scotch Whisky for granted,
assuming, one supposes, that its merits as a drink are self-
evident and that it would be astonishing if everyone did not
wish to drink it. This is an attitude typical of the British
generally, who assume by the same reasoning that our parlia-
mentary and judicial systems are incomparably the best and
are disconcerted when the indigenous peoples of our former
colonies, whom we bullied or cajoled into adopting them,
revert after independence to forms of government and justice
more suited to their temperaments and customs.

It is a view I do not share, so I thought I would try to find
out Chester's reasons for preferring Scotch to American
whiskies, for example, or cognac and other spirits. We began
by talking about the flavour of Scotch, or more accurately the
many subtly different flavours of blended and single malt
Scotches. Soon, imperceptibly, the conversation broadened. I
found myself telling Chester as much about Scotland and the
Scots as about whisky. I described some of the most striking
of the malt whisky distilleries; Tobermory on the island of
Mull standing above Tobermory Bay, whose waters cover one
of the Spanish galleons which sank when fleeing after the
defeat of the Armada; Dalwhinnie, the highest and perhaps
the loneliest distillery in Scotland, which is also an official
meteorological station, where the manager's duties include
measuring the hours of sunshine, the temperature, the rainfall

and, in winter, the snowfalls which frequently cut it off from the rest of the world for a week or more; Edradour, a distillery in miniature which needs only three men to operate it and which stands on the land of the Duke of Atholl, the only man allowed to have a private army.

We talked of history; of how Scots are known to have been making whisky before the end of the twelfth century; of how on the battlefield of Culloden, when Lord Strathallan lay dying, the last rites were administered to him with oatcakes and whisky; of how, in the lawless century that followed, an Edinburgh mob outraged by the execution of a whisky smuggler had rioted and lynched Captain Porteous, the officer commanding the troop of soldiers.

One cannot talk of whisky without speaking of those who make it. I told Chester of Alice Ross, whose father had been head cooper at Glenmorangie distillery for more than sixty years. Alice lived on in the cottage the distillery had provided for him near the cooperage and, past eighty, insisted on cleaning the distillery offices every morning to repay the company's generosity. Then there is Derek Bottomer, manager of Talisker distillery on the Isle of Skye, who for many years was a key figure in the island's mountain rescue team, a band of amateurs who go out in the worst of weathers to save foolhardy climbers on the treacherous Cuillin mountains. I told Chester, too, of the time when Donald Mackinlay, the fifth generation of his family to be a whisky blender, was obliged to have a harmless growth in his nose removed by surgery and spent a week of tortured anxiety until he could return to his sample room and reassure himself that he had not lost the sense of smell that made him a leader in his profession.

Scotch Whisky, however you sip and savour it, has the same disconcerting habit of evaporating, irretrievably, from a

4

glass as it has from the oak casks in which it lies maturing. Our glasses were empty so I ordered two more single malts, 12-year-old Dalmore, partly because Chester had never tasted Dalmore, but also because we had begun talking about another of the most lovable whisky characters, Colonel 'Hac' Mackenzie who for many years had been associated with the distillery on the Cromarty Firth.

Chester held his glass up to the light, admiring the colour of the whisky, as he said, 'Earlier, you asked me why Scotch is my favourite drink.'

'Aye, I did.'

'Since then, you've answered your own question.'

'How so?'

'You've described the beautiful settings in which Scotch is made, you've sketched the character of the people who make it, their skill and patience and dedication. You've given me an insight into the history of the Scots, their customs and traditions. For me, all that is Scotch Whisky and that's why I drink it. Scotch is much more than a drink, it is your heritage. Scotch Whisky is Scotland.'

2

The Water of Life

Those who have been fortunate enough to fly across the west coast of Scotland on a fine day are unlikely to forget the experience. Beneath them in the sea are the Hebrides, two long, overlapping archipelagos, the inner and outer isles, fringing the Atlantic and protecting the coast of Scotland from the fury of its worst storms. The islands, five hundred and fifty in all with sixty-four inhabited, lie like a broken necklace, stretching from north to south for two hundred and forty miles. The sea can be pure sapphire, and in the ever-changing light the colours of the islands vary, ranging from the palest of lime greens to a deep indigo. Seeing them one can sense what the first Norsemen felt when they came more than fifteen hundred years ago and saw so much beauty ready to be plundered.

Islay is the most southerly of the Hebrides. Like all Scottish isles, it has a character of its own. Looking at its contour on a map, one is reminded of a small elephant, sitting haughtily with its back towards not only its neighbouring island of Jura, but towards Scotland itself. At one time there might have been cause for haughtiness. For almost four hundred years Islay and the other Hebridean isles belonged to the crown of Norway, and the Vikings treated Scotland, divided and impotent as it was, with disdain. Not until 1266 did the Hebrides become a part of Scotland again.

Today no one who knows Islay and its people would ever think of them as haughty or unwelcoming. How could they be, when their lives are inextricably linked with whisky? Some people think of Scotch Whisky as a symbol of hospitality. In Scotland it is more than that; the very essence of social life, a dram to be offered to the friend who calls at one's house, several drams to welcome the new year at Hogmanay, a wee drop to wet the baby's head after a christening, a glass to be raised by the President of a great banquet as he gives the toast 'Slainte Vhar'. No occasion, however humble, however majestic, will not be enhanced and uplifted by Scotland's native drink.

Islay has eight distilleries. Arriving at the island by air from Glasgow, as the pilot begins his descent, you will see three of them; clusters of small, white buildings on the edge of a blue sea. The names of the island's distilleries – Ardbeg, Bowmore, Bruichladdich, Bunnahabhin, Caol Ila, Lagavulin, Laphroaig and Port Ellen – will tell you that Islay is at least as Celtic as Norse; when you land, you will hear Gaelic spoken in the shops and the pubs.

On one of my visits to Islay some years ago, I approached it by sea, though not of my own choice. In those days the daily scheduled passenger flight from Glasgow would land briefly at Campbeltown on the Mull of Kintyre to drop off a passenger or two before continuing to Islay. I always found the landing at Campbeltown depressing, mainly because the long, gaunt runway of the airport, built for the use of NATO forces in any emergency, was a permanent reminder of the possibility of nuclear war. Another reason for depression was that on Campbeltown, once thriving with more than thirty distilleries, now only two remain.

On this particular occasion, after landing at Campbeltown, we were told that the plane would not continue its journey to Islay, for the cloud base was too low to permit landing on the island, but would instead return to Glasgow. So the couple of dozen passengers were loaded on to a coach and driven along the coast to West Loch Tarbet, where we would be able to board Macbrayne's ferry, a steamer which sailed to the islands of Islay, Gigha and Jura.

On the drive to West Loch Tarbet, I found myself sitting next to Bruno, a journalist from an up-market magazine published in Milan, who was visiting Scotland to prepare an article on Scotch Whisky. Malt whisky had during the last few years taken Italy by storm. Everyone was drinking it, in night clubs and discotheques and bars and at the parties of the diplomatic corps. Bruno was short and stout and, with his grey hair cut patrician style and a fringe of curls over his forehead, might have been a not fully debauched Nero. Travelling with him was his photographer Monica, a girl of exceptional loveliness.

By the time we had boarded the ferry it was well past midday, and as we sailed, I invited Bruno and Monica to lunch with me in the dining saloon. That would be a nice

8

gesture, offering the Italians a foretaste of the hospitality they would surely be given on Islay. I rationalised it thus, but on reflection I realised that it might have been not a gesture, but a response to Monica's huge brown eyes, which were flashing signals far more compelling than those of the lighthouse on the Rinns of Islay, or so it seemed.

Two good friends of mine were lunching on board that day. George Grant, a distiller from the valley of the Spey, and Duncan Macgregor, production director of the Glasgow whisky firm, Long John Distilleries, had driven to West Loch Tarbet and were taking Duncan's car over to Islay on the ferry. They were sitting at a table next to ours.

The steward of the dining saloon was a brawny fellow, *costaud* was how the French would describe him, but not a great communicator. When we had ordered our lunch – lentil soup with sippets, mince and tatties to follow – wishing to show my Italian guests that even in the west of Scotland we know something of La Dolce Vita, I asked him for the wine list. He made no reply, looked at me for a moment and then strode away. Presently he returned carrying two bottles of wine, one of red and one of white, which he thrust at me.

'There's this,' he said, 'and this.'

Neither George Grant nor Duncan were making any serious attempt to restrain their amusement and I felt like a character from one of those old Bateman cartoons – 'The Man who Asked for the Wine List on the Islay Ferry.'

George leant over from his table. 'Why not offer your guests the wine of the country?' he suggested, and then added, 'They have Glenfarclas on board.'

'*Bravissimo!*' Bruno exclaimed. He may have seen the labels on the bottles of wine.

I sent for a bottle of the malt for the five of us to share; an extravagant gesture, but almost a lifetime of living in England had atrophied my Scottish thriftiness. Glenfarclas was George's distillery and its whisky would be on every connoisseur's list of the top single malts.

When Monica sipped it, she exclaimed, 'But this is nothing like the malt whisky I have tasted at home!'

'What do you drink in Milan?' I asked her. 'Glen Grant?'

'Yes. How clever of you to know!'

In truth my guess had not been very clever, scarcely a guess at all. Glen Grant had been the first single malt Scotch to crack the Italian market, as Americans would say. Its delicate, almost effeminate, bouquet may have been one reason for its extraordinary popularity in Italy, but even more important had been the marketing skills and energy of Armando Giovinetti, the importer whom the Scottish company had chosen to handle it. In the early days Glen Grant had been a *succès fou* in Italy. I recall a reception in the Hotel Flora in Rome where two hundred people, the 'Mondo Nero', film stars, writers, diplomats and even a cardinal or two, were drinking Glen Grant as though the distillery might at any moment run out of supplies, which incidentally it almost did.

'How is it,' Bruno asked me, 'that two malt whiskies can taste so different?'

The question is one that many people ask. Scotland has more than a hundred malt whisky distilleries, and the whisky made in each of them has a flavour of its own. There are a number of reasons for this. The shape and size of the copper pot stills in which malt whisky is distilled is one factor, the amount of peat used in making the malt another. All Scotch Whisky is matured in oak casks, and the type and size of cask used, as well as the length of time for which it is matured, have a bearing on its ultimate flavour. The most important factor, though, without any doubt is the water from which the whisky is made. Every distillery has its own water supply, usually a burn or spring, jealously guarded.

A story which illustrates the crucial role played by water in distilling is that of Peter Mackie, a rich and energetic businessman in Glasgow at the turn of the century. 'Restless Peter', as he was called, felt he had been slighted by the Hunter family, owners of Laphroaig distillery at that time. Laphroaig is the best known of the Islay distilleries and they used to say that at least a little Laphroaig was used in every leading brand of blended Scotch. Restless Peter became raging Peter and he swore he would drive the Hunters out of business by building a distillery which would produce a whisky identical in flavour to that of Laphroaig. He built his distillery a short distance along the coast, fitted it with pot stills that were the same size and shape of those at Laphroaig and imitated every detail of the distilling process. The result was a perfectly good malt whisky, but one with a flavour which was completely different from that of Laphroaig. The reason for this was the water. Mackie had drawn the water for his distillery from the same hills as Laphroaig, but not of course from the same burn.

Over the next day or two, Bruno and Monica would have plenty of opportunities to taste the whiskies distilled in all the eight distilleries on Islay. Each of them has a flavour of its own, but in every one of them one can detect a common character, difficult to describe but unmistakable to anyone who knows his single malts. One might think of them as music, eight orchestral compositions, each one different but with a common motif, subtle and half-concealed, running through all of them.

When finally the ferry reached Islay, the five of us learnt that we were all invited to a ceilidh that evening. Ceilidhs are a part of life on the Western Isles, a cultural heritage of a past when people had to make their own entertainment and not buy it prepackaged in celluloid or plastic cassettes or on a television screen. Not so long ago folk would gather in the evenings round a peat fire in a Tigh Dubh, a rough stone cottage with a thatched roof which housed a man's cattle as well as his family, and entertain each other by telling stories, reciting poems or singing Gaelic songs. That was how the legends and the poems and the songs were handed down, and in a way they still are.

Today, though, ceilidhs are not the same. On the mainland, they have paid performers who give commercialised interpretations of the songs and verses that are Scotland's cultural heritage. On Islay the ceilidhs, though more formal and organised than in the old days, still have a spontaneity and amateurish good humour that are hard to resist. The ceilidh on the evening of our arrival was in honour of Bruno's visit and held in Bowmore distillery.

Bowmore, in the township of that name, is on the shore of Loch Indaal, a sea loch between the elephant's trunk and its body, which almost divides Islay in two. Like many distilleries in Scotland, Bowmore had recently built a visitors' reception centre with a fine hall and it was there that the ceilidh was organised, unobtrusively but efficiently, by 'Happy Harry' Cockburn, the distillery manager. They had a band, led by the milkman on drums with his wife doubling on accordion and piano, which played modern music, interspersed at intervals with the mandatory Scottish dances: the eightsome reel, the Gay Gordons, the Dashing White Sergeant. In between dances, guests sang; Evan Cattanach, assistant manager of a distillery on the island who had won medals at the Mod (Scotland's annual festival of Gaelic music), Mairi, the pretty wife of Grant Carmichael, another distillery manager, and Dougal, the island's postman, who performed some mouth music. A stout lady recited a long poem in English and a wee girl performed a sword dance.

Even Bruno agreed, with no more than a show of reluctance, to sing for us and, with a Neapolitan song, proved he had a fine tenor voice. The enthusiasm of the audience for his performance was in no way diminished by the fact that the milkman's wife, who accompanied him on her accordion, was playing in a key marginally different from the one Bruno had chosen.

The other guests that evening were mainly workers at the distillery and their wives and Islay folk, excise officers, hoteliers, shopkeepers and farmers. They included two people who were local celebrities in their own way. One of them was Bessie Campbell, at that time the owner of Laphroaig distillery and the only woman in Scotland to own – and manage – a distillery. How she became that is a story worth recounting.

Many years previously – it would be unchivalrous to say how many – Ian Hunter, the owner of Laphroaig, wished to engage someone to manage the commercial side of his business. He was a man who liked to spend his time fishing or stalking or playing golf rather than in an office. He may also have been a difficult man, for he could find no one to run his office for him. Bessie's father was a good friend of Hunter and he persuaded his daughter to give up her schoolteaching job in Glasgow and to go and work at Laphroaig, just to help Hunter out, it was agreed, and only for a year. Once on Islay, she fell in love with life on the island and, some said, with Hunter. She was a capable girl and before long was running the distillery. When Hunter fell ill, she took charge completely, and when he died he left the distillery to her.

She stayed on Islay for more than fifty years and became

accepted in the man's world of distilling, as much for her knowledge of whisky as for her charm and kindness. Newspapers christened her 'The Queen of Whisky Island'.

Bessie's maiden name had been Williamson and it had only been recently, at an age when many thought they should have known better, that she had met and married Wishart Campbell. Wishart, a Canadian light entertainer, had come to Islay in search of his ancestral roots and finished up with a wife, a part share in a distillery and a fine house overlooking the sea. A magnificent white grand piano was instilled in the house, on which, when the mood took him, Wishart would accompany himself as he sang those excruciatingly sentimental Irish songs.

Midway through our ceilidh that evening there was an interval for supper. Guests helped themselves from a generous abundance of baps and sandwiches and pies and cakes laid out on long tables. Most of them would not have eaten since the 'tea' they had had on returning home after work, and Scottish dancing sharpens appetites as well as thirsts. I stayed in the bar with Bruno and Bessie Campbell, for we had all dined, Bessie at home and the two of us at our hotel.

Monica was working, photographing everyone and everything, lying full length on the floor or climbing up into the roof beams to find more interesting camera angles. I was able to persuade her to stop working only once during the evening, and that was when she partnered me in an eightsome reel. As one would have expected, she danced superbly, even though she had never heard a reel played before, and I could sense that every man in the ceilidh was watching me enviously.

Bruno, who had tasted Laphroaig single malt back at our hotel, was asking Bessie why its flavour was so much stronger than those of the other Islay malts. 'Stronger' was the expression he used, but he might more accurately have said 'pungent'. In my experience, Laphroaig is a whisky which many people actually dislike when they first taste it. Pat, a golfer friend, once bought a bottle of it in a duty free shop, tasted it when she returned home and immediately gave it to me. She would not even accept payment, but then she is not a Scot, of course. After a time, though, people very often become infatuated with Laphroaig. In other words, like so many of the best things in life, it is an acquired taste.

'We use more peat in our malt kiln,' Bessie explained.

As we had driven through the island earlier that evening, we had passed a peat moss and had stopped to watch the peat being cut. Two men were at work, one in a trench some three feet deep, deftly cutting turves of peat and lifting them up for the other man to stack on the bank. Soon afterwards in Port Ellen, where we were all staying, we had noticed the distinctive smell of peat smoke coming from the chimneys of the cottages.

Malt whisky is made from malted barley. Laphroaig and Bowmore are two of a diminishing number of distilleries in Scotland which make the malt they use in traditional floor maltings. The barley, which is brought in from the mainland, is first soaked in water and then spread over the stone floor of the malt barn, where it will begin to germinate. This takes several days, during which it must be turned at regular intervals to control the rate of germination and the temperature. Two or three men equipped with large flat wooden shovels known as 'shiels', pick up the sprouting grain and toss it in the air. They work as a team, moving across the malting floor with a rhythm almost as graceful as a Highland dance. Sadly, it is a dying spectacle, as more and more of the malt used in distilleries is made centrally in large mechanical maltings.

'When do you use the peat?' Bruno asked Bessie.

She told him that when germination reaches the right stage, releasing the starch in the sprouting grain, it must be stopped. The 'green malt' is dried by spreading it over a wire mesh floor above the malt kiln. Peat is burned in the kiln and its smoke rises through the grain, impregnating it with the 'peat reek', which gives Scotch Whisky its characteristic smoky flavour.

'The kiln is fired with peat to start with,' Bessie explained, 'and the drying finished over coke or anthracite. The amount of peat used determines the flavour of the malt and the smokiness of the whisky.'

While we were chatting in the bar, the other island 'celebrity' who was at the ceilidh that night came and joined us. Sean O'Leary was an Irishman, an artist who had made his home on Islay, living in a caravan just off the road not far from Laphroaig distillery. His reasons for choosing Islay were much the same as those why artists like Picasso, Modigliani and Brancusi went to live in Montmartre at the beginning of the century. Living was inexpensive and the local people tolerated their bohemian way of life, even taking their paintings from time to time as payment for food and wine.

The people of Islay, being Scots, did not carry their tolerance to such lengths of extravagance, but a distillery manager, Hamish Scott of Ardbeg, was once rash enough to commission Sean to paint a huge mural on a bare white wall of the living-room in his house. Sean tackled the assignment with enthusiasm, though no great sense of urgency, painting for many days while Rae, Hamish's pretty, good-natured wife, cooked all his meals and kept him supplied with whisky. The mural, when finished, was spectacular: a Bacchanalian scene with naked maidens gambolling and men

16

carousing by moonlight on one of Islay's beaches. Hamish had been too busy to watch Sean as he worked, and only when the mural was finished did he realise that the 'models' for the mural had been taken from life. Every one of the naked maidens and the tipsy men bore a curious resemblance to one of Hamish's island friends, and the devil who was masterminding the orgy was unmistakably the Minister of one of the churches.

That evening, without too much difficulty, we persuaded Sean to take a dram of Bowmore. He liked to believe that he was something of an expert on the malt whiskies of Islay, and indeed by various expedients he would have managed to taste all of them at one time or another. At that time he was going through a phase of professing a dislike of Lagavulin. The reason for his prejudice was yet another of the island's stories.

He had built himself a canoe out of driftwood, he claimed, and most evenings he would paddle it just off the shore to Port Ellen, hoping he might find a visitor in one of the hotels who would buy his paintings. One night as he returned home, the waves turned boisterous and the canoe foundered. Sean was able to scramble ashore and, by one of those strokes of good fortune which come to the aid of life's survivors, found he had beached only a few yards from Lagavulin distillery. He arrived there, his clothes soaked, his wild white hair bedraggled, still spluttering from the salt water he had swallowed. They took him in, found towels, and allowed him to dry himself in front of the furnaces that heated the pot stills.

'Did you ever hear the like of it afore?' he would afterwards exclaim indignantly. 'It would never happen in Ireland, to be sure. They've thousands of gallons of whisky lying in those warehouses and all they offered me was a cup of tea! Tea!'

As we were drinking, I told Bruno my theory why all Islay Malt whiskies have that distinctive character, the subtle motif to be found in all of them. To me it has always seemed an almost medicinal flavour, with a tinge of iodine in it. Might that not be because Islay is a small island, washed by the sea, drenched by sea spray and often shrouded in a heavy sea mist? Could that subtle flavour be a flavour of the ocean, redolent of salt spray and green seaweed lying beside rock pools? Over the centuries the peat on the island must have been impregnated with that flavour, and through the peat its tang would pass into the malted barley and from the malt into the whisky.

As I was explaining my theory, George Ballingall came to join us in the bar. George and his wife Winnie were old friends, and I had shared many drams and many stories with them in their house by the water's edge across the bay from Port Ellen. George was then an 'inspector' with the Distillers Company Limited, responsible for running the three distilleries it owned on the island.

'I doubt if it can be the peat that gives Islay whiskies their distinctive flavour,' he remarked when I had finished speaking.

'Why not?'

'Some distilleries on Islay use malt which has been brought in from the mainland, where it would have been made with local peat. Their whiskies may be lighter than Laphroaig and Lagavulin, but they're still unmistakably Islay whiskies.'

'Then what is it that gives Islay whiskies that characteristic medicinal flavour?'

'The water would be the principal factor. Don't forget that the water we use in distilling flows through peat, which, as you say, is impregnated with the tang of the sea.'

The best water to use in making Scotch Whisky, I have

heard many distillers say, flows through peat and over granite. Because granite is a hard rock, the water does not pick up any undesirable minerals, and because it flows through peat, it is soft. On Islay one can immediately notice how soft the water is, if not when drinking it, then certainly when washing in it.

We talked for a little longer about the flavour of Islay whiskies, of peat and water and malt and the sea. Sean was becoming impatient with what he probably felt was a sterile, theoretical argument, and the memory of his treatment at Lagavulin distillery still irritated him.

'Of course it's the sea that gives Islay whisky its flavour!' he said dogmatically, banging his empty glass down on the table. 'I should know. I've tasted both!'

Next morning I found myself acting as chauffeur to Monica. When gathering material for an article, Bruno did not like to be accompanied by his photographer. Photographers, he said, needed too much time to set up their shots and he liked to move around talking to as many people as possible. So he and Monica planned their work for the day separately. Bruno was to visit Laphroaig distillery, where he would interview Bessie Campbell, and then go on to Lagavulin and Ardbeg. Monica had arranged to take photographs of the distilling process later in the morning at Caol Ila, for she had heard it was the most photogenic of the distilleries. But first she wanted to tour the island, taking photographs as her whim dictated.

I agreed to drive her in the car I had rented for my stay on Islay. We went to Kildalton first to see the Kildalton Cross, the only surviving complete Celtic High Cross in Scotland which dates back to the eighth century. From there we drove to Bowmore, stopping at the island's toy airport to watch a man in a truck shepherding sheep that had strayed on to the runway to safety before the daily plane arrived. In Bowmore, Monica photographed the round church at the entrance to the village, which had been built in that shape, they say, so that the devil could find nowhere to hide in it. Bowmore itself is one of the earliest examples of village planning in Scotland, constructed in 1768 at the same time as Edinburgh's New Town was being built. Monica stopped people in the streets to photograph them, getting not a single refusal. Her charm and her smile were impossible to resist, as I had already discovered.

Caol Ila distillery is named after the narrow sound which separates Islay from the island of Jura. It was built on the edge of the sound, overlooking the sea and with a wonderful view of the Paps of Jura, the three mountains that dominate the tiny island, rising steeply from the strip of arable land around the coast. The distillery had not long previously been rebuilt and modernised, which makes it ideal for the photographer, who can work without being hampered by a clutter of wood and pipes and overhanging beams. I feel that it has lost a lot of its charm, but it still draws its water from Loch nam Ban over which, in the words of a visitor more than a hundred years ago, 'ever and anon the fragrant breeze from myrtle and blooming heather is wafted'.

George Ballingall and Grant Carmichael were waiting at the distillery to meet us and, after a quick tour of inspection, Monica began to work, taking photographs at the mash tun. In the making of whisky, mashing is the next stage after malting. The malt is ground in a mill and then, in order to extract the sugar, mixed with hot water in a large cylindrical vessel. George and I grew restless as Monica set up her lights and began taking shots of the mechanical stirrers revolving in the mash tun. It was already well past midday, so we left her in the care of Grant and walked from the distillery over the cliffs to Port Askaig, where we had arranged to take lunch.

Port Askaig is dignified with the title of 'port' because it has a landing-stage. It also has a hotel, a shop and a petrol pump, but nothing more. Even so, it is a delightfully pretty spot, nestling at the bottom of a steep hill, facing the sound with Jura beyond.

As George and I sat at the table in the hotel's small garden, enjoying our first dram of the day, we talked of the changes that were taking place on Islay. Only a year or two previously, anyone wishing to visit Jura would have had to rely on Archie McPhee who would ferry people across the sound in his boat. He would make the journey with the gloomy solemnity of a Charon crossing the Styx, but without the same reliability. Anyone who engaged Archie to ferry him over in the morning might well find that he did not return to fetch him later in the day, but left him stranded on Jura for the night. On an island which offers so many congenial alternatives to work – fishing, stalking, sailing, golf or simply watching whisky as it matures – Archie, like many Islaymen, was apt to undervalue the importance of time. People who go to Islay soon find that there is no word in the island's vocabulary as urgent or compelling as *mañana*.

Now, in the interests of progress, Archie has been replaced by a rusty tank landing craft, which must have seen service in the Second World War and takes people and even cars across the sound.

At one time George's company had its own 'puffer' or coastal steamer, which brought barley and empty casks over to Islay, tying up at Caol Ila's own pier and taking casks full of mature whisky back to the mainland. Today there is a drive-on, drive-off ferry service two or three times a day, bringing bulky container vehicles to rumble through the island's roads, brushing the hedges on each side.

Jura has seen changes as well as Islay, and the islanders owe a debt to whisky. Its name in Norse means 'Deer Island', and several thousand deer graze happily on the lower slopes of the Paps, while little more than two hundred people struggle to live from farming tiny crofts, gathering seaweed to make kelp, and fishing, although fishing has never been highly regarded as an occupation on the Western Isles. Until recently the economy of Jura was scarcely viable, although it was unlikely to have suffered the same fate as St Kilda, the pinnacled rock far out in the Atlantic, whose islanders were repatriated to the mainland against their will because the population, reduced from two hundred to forty, no longer warranted the provision of education, medical care and the other social facilities which governments now feel obliged to make available.

Any possibility of this happening on Jura has been dispelled, for it now has a distillery again. The original distillery, built on the island early in the nineteenth century, was abandoned during the First World War, when the restrictions on the sale of drink imposed by Lloyd George were crippling the whisky industry. Only a few years before my visit to Islay, a new one had been constructed as a joint venture by two local landowners and an Edinburgh whisky company. The distillery has brought an extra measure of prosperity to the tiny island community. Even the small number of jobs it offered increased the population by enough to justify enlarging the school and employing a second teacher, and it brought more business to the island's small hotel.

Jura has no police station, or even a resident constable, but is policed from Islay. It does have a reputation for longevity, with records of several inhabitants living past the age of a hundred and one. Mary MacCrain, whose grave can still be seen, died aged one hundred and fifty-six. Whether this is due to the quality of its whisky, or to the absence of police, is a matter only for speculation. Nor do we know whether either of these facts influenced George Orwell to live in a farmhouse on Jura while he was writing *1984*.

In the days of Archie McPhee, people used to say that, although there were a number of cars on Jura, the only ones that were licensed were those belonging to the distillery, the one hotel and the major landowners. Other owners did not license them, for they knew that if the police were coming over to the island from Islay on one of their routine visits, Archie would see that a warning message was telephoned over. Then cars would be hastily put into sheds on the crofts, where everyone pretended they were permanently 'laid up'. Jura folk had a plausible excuse for this socially deviant behaviour. Why should they pay for a road fund licence, they would say, when the island had only one road and the authorities never bothered to repair its surface?

George and I were still talking of Jura that morning when Grant Carmichael brought Monica over the cliffs to the hotel and soon afterwards Bruno arrived to join us for lunch. When he heard that there was a new distillery on Jura, Bruno asked us, 'Isn't building a new distillery a risky enterprise? How can one tell in advance whether the water will be suitable for making a good whisky?'

We agreed that building a new distillery could be something of a gamble, even though one could make tests to indicate the suitability of the water. On Jura, though, the consortium who had built the Isle of Jura distillery had not gambled, for they knew that the previous distillery had produced a whisky which had been highly regarded in the trade. Their confidence was justified, and Isle of Jura single malt whisky soon established its reputation and can be found in bars all over the world. Its flavour, incidentally, in no way resembles Islay whisky, which could be a subject for more passionate argument, but we will let that pass.

'Always one gets back to water,' Monica remarked.

'That may be the reason why whisky got its name; Uisge Beatha is the Gaelic for "Water of Life".'

Bruno, with his journalist's curiosity, had another question for George. 'What, in your opinion, is the finest malt whisky distilled in Scotland?'

George ducked the question with a diplomat's skill. Anyone's opinion of a whisky is purely subjective, he said, a matter of personal taste. All the single malts made in Scotland had their merits and it would be foolhardy to claim that any one of them was the best.

'You may say that,' Bruno replied, 'but I notice that today you are drinking one of your company's whiskies. Yesterday I heard you refuse one of the other Islay malts. Is that just loyalty?'

George smiled. 'Not at all. As George Orwell might have said; All Scotch Whiskies are equal, but some are more equal than others!'

3

River of Gold

Many countries have a region which produces a disproportionate share of their wealth. This may be a Silicon Valley, where computer hard- and software are manufactured or an Aerospace Alley, where the technological marvels of flight and the weapons of extermination are created. Mostly these regions are disfigured by drab factories and faceless people. By contrast, Scotland's golden triangle is to be found in countryside of tranquillity and charm.

The valley of the River Spey does not possess the savage beauty and grandeur to be found in other parts of Scotland, but it has a loveliness of its own. On its way to join the sea in the Moray Firth, the river flows between gently wooded banks and fields where pedigree cattle graze. As one drives along the road from Grantown-on-Spey to Elgin, one can see at intervals on each side of the river small clusters of white buildings with the pagoda roofs of the malt kilns, which tell one that they are not farms but distilleries.

Mistaking a distillery for a farm is not as absurd as it sounds. For centuries most of the whisky made in Scotland was distilled on farms. Almost every farm in the valley of the Spey had a still in which the farmer would use the surplus barley not needed to feed his family and his cattle to make whisky. Today most Speyside distilleries have been built on the sites of these bothy stills. To understand how this cottage craft became an industry which accounts for more than one-quarter of Scotland's export earnings – some £1.7 billion at the latest reckoning – one could do no better than to make one's way to the hub of the Spey valley, the village of Craigellachie.

The tiny Fiddichside Inn stands, as its name suggests, on the River Fiddich, not much more than a stream, just above the point where it flows into the Spey. The owner of what may well be the smallest inn in Scotland is Dorothy Brandie. In spite of her name, Dorothy's life is whisky. Until she inherited the inn from her parents, her husband Joe worked at Macallan distillery which stands on the hill overlooking Craigellachie. Dorothy knows everyone in the closely-knit distilling community on the Spey. On my last visit to the inn only a short time ago, we talked of the father of Evan Catta-nach, whom I first met on Islay but who was then back on Speyside. I mentioned George Grant, who had mocked me on the Islay ferry and whose family owns Glenfarclas distillery. George had retired from the business a short time previously, but Dorothy gave the impression, without actually saying so,

26

that she might have dandled him as an infant on her knee.

Her interest in whisky goes deeper, though, than a mere knowledge of the people on Speyside who make it. Whisky is in her blood. Hanging on a wall in the bar of the inn is an old faded photograph of her grandfather, James Smith of the village of Glass, also known as Goshen, the most famous of the whisky smugglers.

To understand the social phenomenon of whisky smuggling – 'moonshining' would be a more accurate expression – we need to go far back in time. From the time distilling began in Scotland, which we know was at least before the end of the thirteenth century, people made their own whisky. In the Highlands and on the islands it was not a commercial enterprise but a cottage industry, and the government made no attempt to control or restrict it except when a harvest had been exceptionally poor and grain was scarce. From time to time restrictions might be imposed locally, but generally Scotsmen made whisky for their own use freely, and over the centuries came to believe that this was an inalienable right. Then in 1644, the Scottish Parliament, seeking to raise funds with which to maintain an army, passed the Scottish Excise Act, which imposed a duty of two shillings and eight pence per Scots pint – equivalent to about one-third of a gallon – on whisky and other spirits.

There followed two centuries of widespread, almost universal, illicit distilling. Making whisky is a relatively uncomplicated operation. The only basic equipment needed is a vessel in which a fermented mash of cereals is heated until it vaporises. Alcohol vaporises more quickly than water, and the vapour which comes off the vessels is condensed and collected. Because the process is simple, it is also not impossible to conceal.

When they could no longer distil whisky openly in their

bothies, Scots found a way of concealing what they were doing, sometimes in cellars or sheds which could be camouflaged by growing grass or heather on the roofs. More commonly the still would be operated in a hollow on the moors, near a convenient burn which could be used to cool the 'worm' or copper tube in which the spirit was condensed. Smoke from the peat fire used to malt the barley and to heat the still might betray a clandestine outfit to the Revenue Officers, so lookouts, usually women or small children, would be posted. Sometimes flags or sheets would be hoisted to give warning of the enemy's approach. Revenue Officers, or 'gaugers' as they were known, were few in number, with large areas of countryside to scrutinise, and it was rare for an illicit still to be detected, except on information given to the authorities by rival smugglers.

Smuggling led to an alarming decline in morals wherever it was practised. Money could now be made by selling illicitly distilled whisky, and before long it became an organised enterprise. Whisky made in the Highlands was of a much better quality than that produced in and around the cities of the Lowlands. One reason for this was the skill of the distiller, but equally important was the quality of the water. Soon bands of smugglers, usually armed to prevent high-jacking by rival gangs, were taking their whisky on pack-horses or mules to Perth and other cities where it could be sold more or less openly on market days.

Locally ingenious ways were devised to hide stocks of illicit whisky, as on the occasion when it was put into an empty coffin, with a funeral cortege in attendance. In some areas small-scale guerilla warfare developed as smugglers diverted the attention of the Revenue men with false information and spurious tip-offs, which sometimes resulted in assaults and gang fights and, not infrequently, fatalities.

The law became almost impossible to enforce. Revenue men were bribed and magistrates were reluctant to impose more than token penalties on offenders whom they knew to be otherwise law-abiding. On occasions magistrates themselves might be corrupted. There is the story of a woman accused in court of smuggling who told the sheriff, 'I hav'na' made a drop since yon wee keg I sen yourself.' Rewards were offered for information leading to the discovery of an illicit still, but the smugglers even used these to their advantage. The 'worm' or copper tube used to condense the spirit was the most costly piece of equipment needed to make whisky. When this was worn out, smugglers would take Revenue officers to the site of an illicit still, claim the reward of £5 and use it to buy another worm.

The situation was made worse by the large quantities of wine and liqueurs being smuggled in from the continent. Historians have estimated that more than half the population were involved, directly or indirectly, in illicit distillation or smuggling. Early in the nineteenth century attempts were made to combat what was a growing social malaise, by allowing distillation under licence and raising the duty. They failed, and hardly anyone in the Highlands bothered to apply for a licence. In the small parish of Glenlivet alone it was believed that two hundred small stills were being operated. At this point, in 1820, the Duke of Gordon, Laird of Aberlour and one of the biggest landowners in that part of the country, drew the attention of the House of Lords to the deplorable consequences of smuggling in Scotland. On his advice and with his assurance that landowners would do all they could to stamp out illicit distilling, the Excise Act of 1823 was passed by Parliament. This reduced the excise duty and allowed distillation on payment of a relatively modest licence fee, provided stills had a capacity of at least forty gallons.

Penalties for breaking the law were made more severe.

The Act laid the foundations of today's Scotch Whisky industry, even though at the time it aroused fierce hostility in the Highlands. Most of the bothy stills were too small to qualify for a licence and large numbers of people continued to make whisky illegally for their own domestic use. Smuggling continued up to the end of the century and beyond, and even in recent times there has been the occasional isolated discovery of a still in the heather. Being found in possession of a still is an offence which, on conviction, will bring a heavy fine or even imprisonment.

In Elgin, the city at the end of the Spey valley, they tell the story of Willie, a local man who appeared in court accused of illicit distilling. The Sheriff asked the constable who had made the arrest whether he had caught the accused in the act of making whisky. The constable admitted that he had not, but pointed out that he had found Willie with all the necessary equipment. Willie was found guilty, but before sentencing him, the Sheriff asked whether there were any other offences which he would like taken into consideration.

Willie thought for a while. 'Aye, just the one, your honour. Rape.'

'What!' the Sheriff exclaimed. 'Are you saying you have committed rape?'

'No, I hav'na', but I've all the necessary equipment.'

Dorothy Brandie's grandfather Goshen was one of the most renowned of the later smugglers, both for the amount of whisky he distilled and for its quality, which everyone agreed was supreme. Looking at the faded photograph in the Fiddichside Inn, one is impressed with his expression of dignity. He was not the kind of man, one senses, who would ever be associated with anything furtive or unworthy. Contemporary reports suggest that he, like many other folk, believed that making whisky was an innocent and reasonable occupation which only an unreasonably stupid law passed by an unthinking Parliament in the distant south prevented them from enjoying.

Goshen was also, by all accounts, a generous man who never refused anyone a dram of his whisky, even after he had retired from his work as a gamekeeper. In the end it was his generosity, or rather the indiscretion of those who enjoyed it, which led to his arrest. On a visit to Speyside, Sir William Grant, a well-known figure in Scotland but no relation to the whisky Grants of Dufftown, enjoyed Goshen's whisky and in an after-dinner speech in London he boasted of how far superior it was to any whisky that could be bought in the south. Unknown to Sir William, his neighbour at dinner was a senior official of the Customs and Excise, and later in conversation he extracted enough information for local officers at Huntly to identify Goshen as the distiller of the whisky. He was arrested and taken to court, where only the eloquence of his lawyer saved him from prison; he escaped with a £10 fine.

Glenlivet is the name that, for many people has come to be synonymous with Scotch Whisky. In the little glen through which the Livet Water flows on its way to join the Avon and then the Spey, whisky of a special quality has been made for centuries. To ask why would be pointless, for no one could give a finite answer to such a question. Distillers have known it instinctively, which is why there were so many bothy stills in that tiny parish.

One of these stills belonged to George Smith, a farmer who had the acumen to realise that after the Excise Act of 1823 there was no future in illicit distilling, but perhaps very promising prospects for a commercial enterprise. So he took

31

out a license for his bothy still, and rebuilt it to enable him to make whisky of good quality on a large scale.

Not surprisingly his conversion was, in the eyes of his fellow smugglers, unforgivable treachery. The stories of how he was abused and threatened by them as he took his whisky over the mountains to Perth or Edinburgh have become part of whisky legend. The Laird of Aberlour presented him with a pair of pistols with which he could defend himself, and to this day they are on show at the Glenlivet distillery, though it is said that he had cause to use them only once, firing them into the fireplace of an inn as a warning to other smugglers there who were threatening to attack him.

Within a few years his whisky was recognised to be the best in the region, so much so that other distillers who followed his example and turned legitimate began incorporating the name 'Glenlivet' in to their own labels, even though their distilleries might be nowhere near the Glen of Livet.

Until a few years ago the malt whiskies of Scotland were generally treated as falling into four categories: Highland malts made north of an imaginary line drawn from Greenock on the River Clyde to Dundee, Lowland malts coming from south of that line, Islay malts from the Isle of Islay and Campbeltown malts distilled near the town of that name on the Mull of Kintyre. Recently, because only two Campbeltown distilleries remain in operation, blenders have tended to drop Campbeltown malts as a category and treat the two whiskies from that area as Highland malts. At the same time it has become increasingly fashionable to divide the Highland malts into two sub-divisions, Speyside malts and other Highland malts.

My personal view is that one should not read too much into these categories. With the exception of the Islay malts, they do not appear to have any identifiable characteristics of flavour in common. It would be surprising if they did have. Take the case of Speyside malts. At present forty-nine distilleries are given the description. Each one has a different source of water, some stand in wooded areas, others on moorland, others again on mountains and several are situated at a good distance from the River Spey. Between them, they cover an area of many square miles. The range of flavours to be found in the whiskies is also extensive. The division of distilleries into Highland and Lowland was originally made for licensing purposes and not because of any differences in the whiskies. One cannot help thinking that it was adopted and later subdivisions devised largely for the convenience of whisky blenders. That is understandable, but it would be unfortunate if the acceptance of a category of Speyside malts were allowed somehow to diminish the merits of other Highland malts in the perception of whisky drinkers.

Those distilleries which tacked the word Glenlivet on to their names might argue that Glenlivet was a recognisable type of malt whisky, that their whisky fell into the category and was entitled to the description. In retrospect, it is clear that they were only trying to cash in on the reputation of George Smith's whisky and to use the term to enhance the prestige of their own. At the time, the practice became so common in the valley of the Spey that Glenlivet came to be known sarcastically as the longest glen in Scotland.

John Gordon Smith, who inherited the distillery in Glenlivet from his father, went to court in 1888 in an attempt to stop other distillers using the name. He won only a partial victory. In a judgment which now seems totally indefensible, although only his distillery was entitled to be called 'The Glenlivet', others could still use the term if it were hyphenated with their own name. For almost a hundred years several Speyside distilleries did so, but recently most of them have discontinued the practice, preferring very rightly for their whiskies to stand on their own reputations.

The Glenlivet distillery of today is very different from George Smith's original modest establishment, for it has expanded enormously and dominates the glen on whose slopes it stands. The quality of the whisky distilled in it remains superb, however, and over the years it has not only retained its reputation in the valley of the Spey, but acquired an international one.

There is a doggerel verse which runs:

Glenlivet it has castles three,
Drumin, Blaifindy and Deskie,
And also one distillery,
More famous than the castles three.

Whoever composed those lines many years ago spoke truer than he probably realised, for today the castles are no more than ruins, while The Glenlivet Single Malt Scotch Whisky, still known affectionately as 'Smith's Glenlivet', is drunk and appreciated around the world.

Nor far from Glenlivet, along the road to Elgin, is Glenfarclas distillery, one of the few remaining distilleries that are privately owned. J. & G. Grant is the family firm of George Grant, who mocked me that day on the Islay ferry, and he ran the business for many years until a year or two back when he handed over to his son John. Both George and John are enthusiastic curlers and seem ready to travel almost anywhere to play this, the traditional winter sport of distillers and farmers in Scotland. Some years ago they constructed a small floodlit area behind the distillery which can be flooded in winter to allow the workers to curl in the evenings.

George also has a lively but dry sense of humour. Often,

when I visited Glenfarclas, he would show me round the distillery and then take me for a dram to his home, which was no more than a couple of hundred yards away and where John and his wife now live. On one such occasion he set two glasses down on a table, handed me a bottle of Glenfarclas single malt whisky and told me to help myself.

I must have looked surprised, for he then explained, 'It has taken me forty years to realise that this way I save whisky. My guests, through politeness, pour themselves a smaller dram than I would feel obliged to pour them out of hospitality.' He smiled as he added, 'Mark you, I wouldn't make the same offer to any of my friends around here!' Even now I have not decided whether the last remark was intended as a compliment. Incidentally, George reminded me that his grandmother preceded Bessie Campbell as a lady distiller. Apparently when George's grandfather died in 1890, she took over running the distillery.

Glenfarclas is another fine malt whisky. It is rich and full-bodied in flavour, exceptionally so and inclined to sweetness, which may be the reason why it is acceptable at strengths higher than the normal and a favourite among connoisseurs of malt whisky.

If, when leaving Glenfarclas, you turn left towards Grantown and then very soon fork right through the tiny village of Marypark, you drop down a leafy lane to the Spey. You cross it by a narrow bridge at Blacksboat and more often than not you will see people fishing there.

The Spey is one of the three great salmon-fishing rivers of Scotland, the other two being the Tay and the Dee. Most of the fishing rights are owned by landowners with property on one or other of its banks, or by hotels, and a chance to fish the Spey is highly prized. A diamond merchant I know has a standing invitation to fish near Craigellachie for one week every year. He is wealthy enough to travel as far as he wishes, but he thinks of this as the best holiday he could have, even though when he is there he is expected to fish every day from dawn till as long as the light lasts. In return for his endeavours he is allowed to take home one 'courtesy' fish, and should he wish to take more he must buy them after negotiating with the ghillie.

On one visit to Speyside, I had parked my car on the road running from Grantown along the north bank of the river – they call it the scenic route – to rest and admire the view, when two ladies taking a stroll approached. We exchanged the usual courtesies and I realised that they must be French. If their accents had not betrayed that, their dress surely would have done. Elegantly robed, beautifully coiffured, they looked a little incongruous walking along a rough country road in stylish, fragile shoes from Rue St-Honoré. They told me that they and their husbands were staying in a large country house that had recently been converted to a hotel. They seemed contented with the arrangement by which their husbands spent all day fishing, while they tested the efficacy of their expensive skin lotions against the ravages of Scotland's midges. When I heard what they were paying for this piece of masochism, I winced.

Visitors to the Spey valley, seeing distilleries on its banks, often ask whether the river suffers any pollution from their proximity. Distillers have always taken the greatest care to protect the environment. As long ago as 1910 a Royal Commission reporting on river pollution commented favourably on the efforts the whisky industry had taken to prevent polluting the rivers of Scotland. Any effluent from a distillery discharged into the river must first be passed through a treatment plant to remove any substance which might reduce the oxygen levels in the water or harm river life in any way. The standards laid down by the River Purification Boards are rigorous, but the industry has always met them. In actual fact, as one would expect in a country noted for its thrift, there is little waste in making whisky. The spent grain after mashing is sold to farmers as cattle food, and the effluent from the stills, which contains nutritious solid matter, is converted in specially constructed plants into 'dark grains' and used to feed poultry.

A little way above the bridge at Blacksboat, a small lane leads to two distilleries, Tamdhu and Knockando. In origin their names have a similarity, both being derived from the Gaelic. 'Dhu' means 'black' as in Tigh Dubh, a black house. 'Tam' is a rock, and 'knock' or 'cnoc' a small hill. Although they stand two minutes' walk apart, the whiskies they make are in no way similar.

Tamdhu may well be the only distillery in Scotland now making all its own malt. Even at Laphroaig the malt made at its floor maltings is supplemented with some bought from professional maltsters. At Tamdhu, malt is made in Saladin or box maltings. The process is essentially the same as in floor maltings, except that the malt is turned mechanically. After being steeped, the barley is filled into long rectangular boxes with brick walls. A device resembling a moving bridge, from which are suspended a number of spiral turners, travels slowly from one end of the box to the other. As it does, the turners rotate, turning the sprouting grain in a different manner from the way maltmen do, but equally effectively. When germination is complete, the green malt is dried over a kiln with some peat used to impart the characteristic smoky flavour.

Knockando would not claim to be one of the oldest malt whisky distilleries in Scotland, but even so it was built as long ago as 1898. Like the majority of malt whisky distilleries today, it buys its malt from professional maltsters, but in all other respects it is not unlike Tamdhu; the distilling process is the same and both distilleries have the traditional low stone warehouses in which the whisky is matured. In both distilleries the malt is ground in a mill into grist, which is fed into the mash tun, so that the sugar can be extracted, exactly as Monica photographed it at Caol Ila.

The next stage in making whisky is fermentation. The sugary liquid or 'wort' from the mash tun is filled into huge cylindrical vats, known as 'washbacks', which can hold fifty thousand litres or more. Yeast is added and almost at once it begins to work, converting the sugar in the wort into alcohol. The violence of the reaction is startling, and the wort begins to foam and bubble, rising up the washback to a point when rotating switch blades are needed to cut off the head and prevent it spilling over the top of the vessel. Eventually the violence subsides, the yeast is spent, and we are left with a cloudy liquid, not unlike a kind of beer, known as 'wash'.

The washbacks at both Tamdhu and Knocando are made of wood. This is traditional, either larch or Oregon pine usually being used, but several distilleries have installed washbacks made of stainless steel. Washbacks have to be cleaned after every fermentation – this is vital – and at some distilleries they are still cleaned by scrubbing the sides and bottom with besoms made of heather as they are hosed down. Stainless steel is much easier to clean than wood, and advocates of steel washbacks maintain that they give better control over the fermentation. This is an oversimplification of an argument which can never be resolved and, as we shall see, there are many such controversial issues in the making of Scotch Whisky.

Telling the difference in flavour between the whiskies

made at Tamdhu and Knockando is simple enough. Finding words to describe their flavour and character is much more difficult, for different people would use different adjectives for the same whisky. Perhaps at this stage one should do no more than say that Knockando is certainly lighter to the taste than Tamdhu, though no one could possibly suggest that the latter is heavy or robust. The point to remember is that they are the types of whisky that those who own and run the distilleries wish to make, and who can say that their judgment is wrong?

The two distilleries do enjoy one characteristic in common, and a felicitous one: their situation. Both stand just above the Spey with glorious views across the hills. Below them the river flows, not lazily but unhurriedly, as though taking its tempo from the ancient craft it has nurtured in its valley, the slow, leisurely craft of making the best whisky.

Making good whisky needs a source of pure, cool water and soft, clear air in which the spirit can lie as it matures. For this reason most Scotch Whisky distilleries are to be found in remote, rural areas, where they have become small communities, with the workers and their families living in cottages provided by the distillery owners. Both Tamdhu and Knockando match this description and so does Cardhu, a few minutes' walk up the road, where there is a school and a kirk as well.

In its early days Cardhu was owned by Elizabeth Cumming, who preceded both Bessie Campbell and George Grant's grandmother as the first woman to run a distillery. Elizabeth was the widow of Lewis Cumming, whose father John had in 1813 become tenant of the farm of Cardhu which, because of its remote location, was ideally situated to distil illegally. Another asset it possessed was an ample supply of spring water and peat. A licence had been taken out for the distillery in 1824 but it remained part of the farm, and when her husband died in 1872, Elizabeth was left with both as well as three young children. She engaged men to help her and managed the business for seventeen years with energy and resourcefulness. In 1893 she sold the distillery, which had been greatly enlarged, to the wine merchants, John Walker & Sons of Kilmarnock, who were to become famous throughout the world for their blended Scotch Whiskies. Elizabeth Cumming, one might say, founded a whisky dynasty. Her grandson Ronnie, later Sir Ronald Cumming, became chairman of both the giant Distillers Company Limited and of The Scotch Whisky Association.

A huge, genial man, Ronnie Cumming played rugby for Scotland and golf whenever he could find the time, although he was by no means of international class at that game. His good nature and tact made him a first-class chairman, but like all of us he had his frailties. One of his was that he was a terrible, but terribly eager, raconteur who massacred any number of good stories wherever he went, usually laughing so immoderately as he told the joke, that he either forgot the punchline or made a mess of it.

There was the occasion when, as chairman, he presided over the opening ceremony of new offices and an exhibition centre which The Scotch Whisky Association had founded in Half Moon Street in London, where incidentally Conan Doyle's Professor Moriaty was supposed to have lived. The then President of the Board of Trade, Douglas Jay, was the principal guest at the opening and set things off to a bad start, when he let it be known privately that he never drank whisky and asked that a glass of sherry should be procured for him. Ronnie was to make a speech, reminding everyone of the very considerable achievements of Scotch Whisky, the exports of which were at the time increasing by almost ten per cent a year.

A team of writers, of whom I was one, had been asked to prepare a suitable speech, and Ronnie told us that he would like to end on a light-hearted note. At functions arranged by The Scotch Whisky Association all whisky offered to guests is served in decanters, simply for diplomatic reasons, so that no member of the Association might feel that the brands of other members but not his were being given the benefit of any publicity that might result. The joke we inserted at the end of the speech was to explain the reason for the decanters and to assure the members that the whisky they would be drinking was certainly not 'even Half Moonshine'. Not the most brilliant of puns, I agree, but it floored Ronnie, even though he was supposed to have read through his speech before the day.

When he came to that part of the text, he stopped and stared at the paper in disbelief. Then he said indignantly, 'It says here that half of what we're drinking is moonshine. That's not true! No one distils illegally in Scotland any more.' Then he added, 'Anyway I know for a fact it's Bell's.' He had no way of knowing what whisky was being served that day but, gentleman as he was, gave the plug to his company's greatest rival.

Poor raconteur though he may have been, Ronnie Cumming was thoughtful and farsighted. Year after year when he was Chairman of The Scotch Whisky Association he used to interrupt his annual report to tell the members that in his opinion the industry was making too much whisky. Unfortunately, people did not listen to his warning, but events showed that he was right.

On my last visit to Cardhu only a short time ago, I discovered that Evan Cattanach, whom I first met years previously when he was assistant manager at Lagavulin distillery on Islay, was now in charge at Cardhu. He showed me round the still house, which is one of the most impressive of any distillery, its six large copper pot stills highly burnished, the walls and floors immaculately clean. The distilling process is the same as the one whisky smugglers were using two hundred years ago, but on a much larger scale.

In a modern malt whisky distillery the fermented wash from the washbacks is distilled twice, a luxury which few of the old smugglers, harassed by the Revenue Officers, would have had the time to enjoy, but undesirable flavouring constituents have to be removed from the spirit. The wash is first heated in a wash still to the point when the alcohol in it vaporises. The vapour passes up the still and is then cooled and condensed. The distillate, known as 'low wines', is then passed to a spirit still and distilled a second time. Even the spirit from this second distillation is not all of the standard required. The first runnings from the still, the 'foreshots', are of neither the right strength or quality, nor are the last runnings, known as 'feints'. Only the middle cut of this second distillation is run into the spirit receiver, from where it will be filled into casks for maturation. The foreshots and feints are collected separately and added to the next batch of low wines from the wash still to be distilled again.

At one end of the still house in Cardhu stands a glass-fronted spirit safe through which one can watch the spirit as it flows from the stills. Instruments enable the stillman to test its temperature and specific gravity and this, together with his visual judgment, allows him to decide the precise moment when the spirit is ready to be collected.

The timing of his decision is crucial to the final quality of the whisky. So exacting is the standard of quality expected in

Scotch Whisky that only a small proportion of the distillate from the spirit still is collected, usually not more than one-third and in some cases as little as 15 per cent. Obviously the more that can be collected, the lower will be the cost of production, and the temptation to run the still a little longer before stopping collection must be strong. To succumb to that temptation will only result in a debasement of the final quality of the whisky. Distillers are courteous by nature and will very seldom comment adversely on another distiller's whisky, preferring to keep their opinions to themselves. Sometimes, though, they can be persuaded or provoked into being critical and then the most common criticism of a malt whisky will be that it is 'too feinty' – in other words, the collection of the spirit has been allowed to continue for too long.

The spirit safe at a distillery is kept locked, so the instruments used to test the new spirit must be controlled remotely. The vessel in which the spirit is collected is also kept locked, and so are the warehouses in which it will be left to mature, to satisfy Her Majesty's Customs and Excise that no spirit is being spirited away without the excise duty being paid. In every distillery Excise Officers, 'the cursed horse leeches of the excise', as Robert Burns described them, are never far away. One might well observe, in parentheses, as it were, that Burns, when unable to support his wife, his family and his mistresses by farming, himself served as an Excise Officer. Poachers are said to make the best gamekeepers, but one may doubt whether poets are the best guardians of the national revenue. Would Dylan Thomas ever have been employed as an Excise Officer in a brewery? The thought is intriguing.

Evan Cattanach still sings and has become an international personality, travelling to all parts of the world to appear on television and radio, wearing his kilt, singing songs by Robert

Burns and talking about whisky. My last visit to Cardhu was in a January, and he arranged for me to be invited to two Burns Night Suppers. The first was in the village hall at Fogwat on the road between Elgin and Aberlour. You might think that an odd and ugly name for a village in such beautiful countryside, but a kind of mist, if not actually a fog, hangs over the place on Burns Night and other occasions of national celebration. The hall was packed with villagers, women as well as men, all enjoying the haggis and the whisky and the entertainment, even though some of the jokes told by the speakers were enough to make any good Presbyterian turn pale.

The other supper, held the following night, was a much more extravagant affair held in a hotel in Fraserburgh. Over two hundred members of the Fraserburgh Burns Club and their guests had gathered for the supper, about half of them in dinner jackets and the remainder in kilts. Evan was to sing, and he had taken Bill Brian, a fiddler who would play. I arrived with them, and the pianist must have assumed that I too was going to contribute to the entertainment.

'What do you do?' he asked me. I murmured that I wrote a bit. 'You can write as much as you like,' he said, rather truculently I thought, 'but if you're going to sing, I have to know what key you wish me to play in.'

I did not sing, but Evan did; two songs of poems by Burns. As far as I can recall they were 'My Luv is Like a Red, Red Rose' and 'Flow Gently, Sweet Afton, among the Green Braes'. Bill Brian is an outstanding fiddler who not long previously had won the Golden Fiddler award presented by a Scottish newspaper. I can only recall one of the tunes he played, and that was 'Music of the Spey'. The toast to the Immortal Memory of Robert Burns given by a local schoolmaster was brilliant, and enough whisky had been placed on the tables to see us through all the 220-odd lines of 'Tam O'Shanter' which the member who recited it every year was certain to give us, unless he had been forcibly restrained. So it was a memorable evening.

Leaving Cardhu and travelling eastwards, presently one reaches the township of Archiestown. The road runs straight and unswervingly between the two rows of sombre, grey houses, a hotel and a general store, offering no temptation to stop. Rather the reverse is true and I have always felt that there is a sinister aura about the township, the ghost of some grisly deed in the past, murder or treachery perhaps, never wholly to be forgotten. It needs only a touch of imagination to see Archiestown as a Scottish counterpart of those menacing towns in the prairies of America that are used as locations for violent films like *Bad Day at Black Rock*.

It is just superstition, but I can always picture torture and evil rites being carried on behind those faceless windows. Yet I know that instead of hurrying through Archiestown, I should stop, dispel the nightmare by taking a dram in the hotel with Highland folk, as direct as the road but courteous and helpful, with a natural dignity one can find nowhere else in Britain. I know I should stop, but on scores of journeys I never have.

You will scarcely have time to shake off the frisson of fear that Archiestown provokes before you pass the entrance to Macallan distillery. There you must stop, for at Macallan they distil a very special malt whisky with a full, rich flavour. I have always believed that if every distiller in Scotland were to be stranded, not on a desert island but in a shepherd's hut on a desolate moor, and was allowed to take two bottles of malt whisky with him, his own and one other, that at least eight out of ten would choose Macallan. For years it was allowed to remain a connoisseur's single malt, largely unknown except

45

to the cognoscenti. In the still house there were only six copper pot stills, modest in size, which limited the amount of whisky that could be produced. Since that time the demand for Macallan has increased dramatically, and so has production. Now the distillery has no less than twenty-one stills, all of the same size and shape as the originals.

People of an inquiring mind might well ask if all pot stills are made of copper, and the answer is that they are. One reason is that copper is easier to shape than other metals, but more importantly it has been shown that there is a chemical reaction between the copper and the spirit which plays an important role in producing a spirit of the right character. The shape and size of the still are also important in determining the ultimate flavour of the whisky, and when a pot still is worn out, it is invariably replaced with one of exactly the same shape and dimensions. At one time, they say, distillers were so concerned about this that they would go to the length of having any dents which over the years might have been made in a still also reproduced exactly. Similarly, any mould or cobwebs that had accumulated in the still house were never removed, in case this too might affect the flavour of the whisky. Today these old traditions are often dismissed by scientists as superstitions in an ancient craft. No doubt they very largely were, but there may have been an element of truth in them. More and more one finds that in a surprising number of instances science eventually discovers that there is a basis of truth in old-fashioned beliefs, for example in old wives' remedies for common ailments.

The man most responsible for the renaissance in the fortunes and status of Macallan among single malts has been Allan Shiach. As a young man Allan did not choose to go into his family's firm which owns the distillery. Instead, after taking a degree at McGill University in Montreal, he went into the entertainment business, becoming a presenter on television in Los Angeles. He also wrote film scripts and was author or co-author of the screenplays of a number of successful films, including *Don't Look Now*, the eerie Daphne du Maurier story set in Venice.

His brother Peter was running Macallan, and when he died at an early age, Allan returned to Scotland and became chairman of the company. He is also, incidentally, a trade unionist and rather proud of the fact. The union, if it can be called such, of which he is also currently the chairman, is the Writers Guild of Great Britain and it is affiliated to the TUC. Since his return to Scotland, the reputation of Macallan whisky has spread at an astonishing speed, aided by shrewd advertising and promotion, which must surely owe a good deal to Allan's imagination and flair. By Madison Avenue standards the advertising campaign is relatively modest, few big colour pages in flashy magazines, but small, almost tongue-in-cheek, advertisements, inconspicuously placed. The intention is to give the customer who then purchases a bottle of Macallan eighteen-year-old single malt the impression that here is a wonderful, almost unknown, whisky that he has discovered for himself.

Allan has many talents. A few years ago three or four of us were in the saloon of a sumptuous yacht, the property of a Wall Street millionaire, in which we were to take a party of celebrities and media people for an evening 'Scotch and Sail' up the Hudson River. We were waiting for the guests to arrive when suddenly Allan sat down at the piano in the saloon and accompanied himself as he sang 'Ave Maria' in a fine, light tenor voice. Twenty minutes later he was performing with equal panache, lecturing an audience of journalists on the mysteries of Scotch Whisky.

*

The valley of the Spey is Grant country, although the Gordons might dispute that they have an exclusive right to it. One can find Grants engaged in all trades and professions – doctors, lawyers, coppersmiths and farmers – and distilling has at least its share. A short distance from Macallan in the village of Rothes, which should not be confused with the New Town of Glenrothes some distance to the south, one will find four distilleries, one of which was founded by Grants.

In 1840 two brothers, James and John, built a distillery which came to be known as Glen Grant and which can be reached at the top of the winding lane at one end of the village. Major John Grant, a son of one of the founders, who took over the distillery, would lead visitors up a path at the back where there was a bridge over the burn from which water for distilling was, and still is, drawn. There he had cleverly contrived for a safe to be built into a rock above the burn to hold a decanter and glasses, so that when his guests had struggled along the muddy path, he could reward them with a dram. The safe is still there, and visitors today may be fortunate enough to be given the same hospitality.

Glen Grant is one of the palest of malt whiskies, almost lemon yellow in colour, and it has a delicate aroma and flavour. This was the single malt which Monica the photographer had drunk in Milan. Malt whisky was scarcely known in Italy until J. & J. Grant appointed Armando Giovinetti as its agent in that country. In a short time sales of Glen Grant began to increase rapidly, until they reached a point when they exceeded those of all but a handful of blended Scotches, a phenomenal achievement. People have suggested that its appeal to Italians was largely due to its colour, which was not unlike the colour of their own aperitif drinks, and it was usually poured over a good many ice-cubes, which would help to conceal its strength. At one point a five-year-old Glen

Grant was being sold in Italy. One can only speculate on whether this was a deliberate strategy to widen its appeal to Italians or whether the move was forced on the company by a shortage of stocks of mature whisky resulting from the unexpected demand. Traditionalists disapproved, believing that no single malt Scotch can be ready to drink after only five years in the cask, but the maturation of whisky is an esoteric subject, one which even scientists do not appear fully to understand and certainly one about which it is dangerous to be dogmatic.

Those who wish to broaden their knowledge of Speyside malt whiskies should make a detour away from the banks of the river. A good path to follow would be the Speyside Way just across the River Fiddich from Dorothy Brandie's inn. The path, which follows what used to be a railway line, passes through lovely countryside and to encourage visitors to use it, it is signposted. In the days before Dr Beeching took his axe to Britain's railways, one could travel by rail from Elgin on a line that meandered through the valley of the Spey to Avie-more. At a number of places there were halts where the train would stop on request to pick up or set down passengers, but the line was mainly used by distilleries. One could see the train passing at a gentle pace, its open waggons piled high with whisky casks, a constant reminder of the leisurely occu-pation on which the prosperity of the valley depends. Many distillery managers believe that Dr Beeching acted in unwise haste, and that if the railway still existed, it would be viable commercially, as well as sparing country lanes their violation by huge, aritculated trucks.

The Speyside Way leads one through lovely countryside to Dufftown, about which there is also an old rhyme:

Rome was built on seven hills,
Dufftown was built on seven stills.

Even though Dufftown now has eight distilleries, no one can dispute that claim. Some fifteen hundred people live in the town and it has been calculated that one-third of this figure is accounted for by distillery workers and their families. Added to their number are all those working in small businesses – builders, carpenters, painters, coppersmiths – who depend almost entirely on the custom of the whisky trade for their livelihood, which would not exist at all if there were no distilleries. In short, Dufftown is a whisky town.

When visiting the valley of the Spey I usually stay at the Craigellechie Hotel, which has the good sense to offer not only the delicacies of nouvelle cuisine, beautifully cooked, but a traditional Scottish menu of a hundred years ago. So ample are the portions that they satisfy even the appetites of those who have been fishing all day. The hotel is a favourite with anglers, and there can be few better consolations for the one that got away than to sample some of its generous selection of single malts in the comfortable bar at the end of the day.

On one visit there I met a Danish author who was collecting material for a book on Scotland. In conversation, he remarked that everyone he met in the valley of the Spey seemed to be either a Grant or a Gordon. The next morning we drove to Dufftown together and I took him to Glenfiddich distillery, where we were fortunate enough to find that the chairman of the company which owns the distillery was there that day. When I introduced the Dane to Sandy Grant Gordon, I think he suspected that I was pulling his leg.

Sandy's great-grandfather William Grant, the son of a tailor who had fought with the Gordon Highlanders at Waterloo, was working for the owners of Mortlach distillery which is also in Dufftown, when in 1886 he set out to build one of his own. With the help of his sons, Glenfiddich was constructed and has remained in the ownership of the Grant family ever since. Today Sandy's son and daughter both work for the firm of William Grant and Sons, as do his brother Charles and Charles's two sons. The company also owns Balvenie distillery just down the road from Glenfiddich, and has now built a third in Dufftown. Kininvie, the new distillery, has only recently started distilling, so its whisky will not be available for some years.

The family's attitude to whisky is epitomised in a story Sandy tells of the occasion when his grandparents were celebrating their golden wedding. His grandfather was offered a glass of champagne, tasted it and was not impressed. 'Take away that fizzy lemonady stuff,' he said, 'and give me a dram.'

With that background you would expect Sandy to hold traditional views, and he is in many ways an archetypal Highland Scot. A leader in the community affairs of the village in which he lives, he is keenly interested in wildlife and hill walking. Any mountain in Scotland over 3,000 feet is known as a Munro, after Sir Hugh Munro, who first listed them. There are 277 of them, and the last time I saw Sandy he told me that he had climbed them all, finishing two years previously with Ben More during a family expedition to the island of Mull.

Not surprisingly, his company believes in the traditional way of making whisky. At Glenfiddich the washbacks are made of wood, not stainless steel, because in his view when the wort is fermenting there is a biological relationship between it and the wood. Some other distilleries have increased the size of their pot stills to meet the growing demand for malt whisky. At Glenfiddich the stills are exactly the same size and shape as the original stills installed by William Grant more than a hundred years ago, and they are heated by coal. The way in which pot stills are heated is

51

another of the controversial issues in the making of whisky.

At one time all stills were heated by coal fires, and it was only in the last few decades that many distilleries began switching to steam heating. Steam is cleaner to use, and those who believe in it also claim that it gives a more even heat and more accurate control. Recently some of those distilleries have been reverting to coal firing because they found that steam heating altered the flavour and the character of their whisky. That is a simplistic explanation of a complex technical matter, and if anything is certain, it is that this and the other debates about the distilling of Scotch Whisky will continue. Neither side in the debate will ever be proved right or wrong, because malt whiskies have in any case changed over the years, not necessarily because of technical changes in the methods of distillation, but because the owners of the distilleries decided to adapt the character of their whiskies to suit what they perceived to be changes in public taste. Lovers of malt whisky should be glad that how to distil the best whisky is still a matter of opinion and leaves room for debate. Every malt whisky has its own style and individuality and any move towards introducing uniformity should be discouraged.

Both Glenfiddich and Balvenie distilleries use water from the same source, the Robbi Dubh spring in the Conval hills. Not only is it important to have the right water for distilling, but that water must never be polluted or contaminated in any way, since this would ruin the whisky. Not long ago, to protect their water, William Grant and Sons purchased 1,000 acres of land around the spring, a whole hillside.

One need scarcely mention that the whiskies produced at Glenfiddich and Balvenie bear no resemblance to each other. To my mind, both are comparatively mild in character, which may be the reason why many connoisseurs believe that Glen-

fiddich in particular is the ideal choice with which to introduce Scotch malt whisky to anyone who has never before
tasted it, and it can claim to be the most widely drunk malt
whisky in the world markets. At the same time, this mildness
is in one way surprising. Old men with long memories who
have been brought up in distilling, and others who write
about it, claim that the traditional malt whiskies of a hundred
years ago and more were much stronger and richer in flavour
than the malts of today. This they say is due to changes in
methods – for example using less peat or even no peat at all
in malting – which have been introduced to meet changes in
taste and lifestyles. The kind of malt whisky best appreciated
after a day spent in the driving rain of the Highlands,
whether rounding up sheep on the hills or stalking deer,
would be too heavy to drink at a cocktail party in a centrally
heated apartment in Manhattan. Now one can find few
distilleries in Scotland more traditional in their methods than
Glenfiddich and Balvenie; particularly Balvenie, which even
the sales literature of the company has described as 'a
museum piece'. Yet no one could possibly find either whisky
robust or pungent in flavour.

My personal preference has always been for Balvenie,
which I believe is one of the finest of the Speyside malts.
Unfortunately, because it is a small distillery and production
is limited, Balvenie can be hard to find. One day I was
lunching at a pub in Edinburgh's Royal Mile and, wishing to
take a malt whisky with my coffee, went to the bar to see
what selection was on offer. In a row of single malts, half
concealed, was a bottle of Balvenie. The barman was a young
man, a student working in his vacations, and when I ordered
Balvenie, he smiled. I asked him then if he had much demand
for it.

He shook his head. 'No,' he replied, 'I don't encourage it.

Balvenie is my favourite dram, and I always have one when I finish work at night. But it's hard to procure, you understand.'

The other distilleries in Dufftown have not achieved the same reputation as Glenfiddich and Balvenie, but one which has always been a favourite among those who really know malt whisky is Mortlach. Until Glenfiddich was built, Mortlach was the only distillery in Dufftown, having been licensed in 1823, the year of the Excise Act. The company which owns it, the United Distillers Group, also owns many other malt distilleries and markets six single malts in its Classic Malt range. Mortlach is not included in the six, and many people find this extraordinary. For years, distillers in the Highlands have spoken of Mortlach with respect and even a touch of envy, and I have always heard it described as a classic Speyside malt, although I have had few opportunities to taste it except when visiting the distillery or in bottlings put out by independent bottlers. When drinking whisky one usually has what can be described as an after-taste, a flavour which lingers on the palate after the whisky has been swallowed. In the case of some single malts, this after-taste is relatively bland and leaves no great impression. The after-taste I have always had when drinking Mortlach is full and well balanced. The smokiness associated with a well peated malt is there, but is not in any way obtrusive.

A few miles to the north of Dufftown in the ancient borough of Keith are five distilleries, with a sixth not far outside. Two of these, Glen Keith and Strathisla, belong to the Canadian company, Seagram Distillers. Strathisla, which has been beautifully restored, can claim to be the oldest operating distillery in Scotland, for it was licensed, though under the name of Milton, in 1786 with one still of forty gallons' capacity. It passed through two or three ownerships until Seagram Distillers bought it in 1950. The story of its acquisition caused much amusement in the valley of the Spey.

Jimmy Barclay, a native of Banffshire, had been an office boy in Benrinnes distillery and had also worked for 'Restless Peter' Mackie, before setting up his own business as a whisky merchant and broker. He established international connections, particularly in North America, and exploited Prohibition by smuggling Scotch into the States through a small island near the border with Canada. When Strathisla was put up for auction in Aberdeen, Jimmy was asked to bid for it on behalf of Seagram.

He had formed the view that £70,000 would be a fair price to pay, but was afraid that local distillers, knowing that he was representing a wealthy North American company, might well gang up on him to force the price well beyond that figure. When the auction stared, he opened the bidding but soon retired, with a great show of disgust, suggesting that the price had climbed too high. Immediately the rival distillers grew suspicious. Jimmy, they knew, would have done his homework. Had he found out something about Strathisla which they had not heard? Perhaps he knew that the water source was inadequate to allow for any expansion of distilling. The bidding petered out, and eventually the distillery was knocked down to a man whom nobody recognised for £71,000. Only later did people learn that the mystery man was a church organist in Aberdeen, a personal friend of Jimmy Barclay, who had paid him a modest stipend to come to the auction and bid on behalf of Seagram.

As a single malt whisky Strathisla is underrated, perhaps because supplies appear to be limited and a very large proportion of what is distilled is used to the company's Chivas Regal blend. It is on sale in very few places, and I always looked forward to visiting Ivan Straker, a former company chairman, in his London office, for one could always rely on him to pour a dram of 15-year-old Strathisla. Ivan was the man who 'saved the Grand National' steeplechase by persuading his company to sponsor it. He is a most likeable, extrovert character, and everyone in the whisky world was full of sympathy for him when his own horse, having led over the last fence, was narrowly beaten into second place in the National.

Strathisla is a delicate malt and people are apt to describe it as a woman's whisky. This is in no way a pejorative comment – not in Scotland, anyway, where whisky has always been a drink to be enjoyed by women as well as men and one could argue that women are as likely as men, if not more so, to have a discerning palate.

A couple of miles outside the town to the north is a distillery which has remained curiously anonymous. One hears its name, Aultmore, mentioned only seldom in conversation even among whisky folk, and yet as far as I know its whisky has been available as a single malt for some years. Smooth and mellow, it is slightly sweeter than the other whiskies made in and around Keith and an ideal malt to drink after dinner.

Also a few miles outside Keith but in the direction of the Spey is Auchroisk distillery. Built only as recently as 1974, it has a silhouette very different from those of traditional distilleries. When it first appeared on a green field site, local people used to say it looked like a cathedral, and certainly the buildings have a lofty grandeur, but they were cleverly landscaped, and over the years as the trees planted around it have grown, Auchroisk has gradually been embraced by the countryside.

A few years ago, presumably as soon as supplies of mature

whisky of a suitable age became available, the owners of the distillery, Justerini and Brooks, decided to bottle its whisky as a single malt. Why not, for although it always seems to me to be a trifle on the light side in flavour, there are many drinkers who would prefer this newcomer to some of the more robust Highland malts which assault the palate without finesse. Variety of choice is the great virtue of Scotch malt whisky. One difficulty facing the marketing men who launched the new single was the distillery's name, for the correct Gaelic pronunciation requires an unusual manipulation of one's vocal chords. People used to complain that it was not so much a name as a throat disease, and one heard many versions, the most common of which was 'Oh, Christ'. So the malt was bottled, primly, as 'The Singleton'. Quite right, too. We all know that whisky is a gift from God, but a blasphemous name would not be appropriate for a whisky distilled in a cathedral!

Returning to the Spey, there are a number of distilleries along or close to its banks which we are by-passing or ignoring in our journey. Some of them may not be of any great historical interest or be especially picturesque, but still produce fine malt whisky. Ben Rinnes is a mountain just to the south of the River Spey, and it would be surprising if the distillery of that name which stands on its slopes did not produce good whisky, for no less than eleven of the distilleries in the Spey valley draw their water from burns or springs on the mountain. Benrinnes is the only Highland distillery which uses triple distillation, but as far as one can tell that does not give its whisky any specially distinctive character. Not far from it is Aberlour distillery, now part of Pernod Ricard, the French drinks group. Scotland and France have been close friends ever since the days of the 'Auld Alliance', but Aberlour is moon miles away in flavour from the aniseed drinks which are the French company's most popular brands. Having said that, I have known people say that they can detect a flavour of mint in Aberlour single malt, though for me its hint of sweetness is not one of herbs but of heather honey.

Whisky blenders, by virtue of their calling, have an exhaustive knowledge of single whiskies, and two whom I know well rank Cragganmore and Longmorn among the best single malts from the valley of the Spey. Cragganmore, in Ballindalloch, is said to have been the first distillery sited to take advantage of railway transport, and when it was built in 1869 it was given its own private siding on the Speyside railway. Ironically John Smith, who founded Cragganmore, was so large in stature that he was forced always to travel in the guard's van of a train. He was too gross to be able to pass through the doors of passenger carriages. Longmorn, further north on the main road to Elgin, is younger than many Spey-side distilleries, having been built only just before the beginning of the century. Its whisky, bottled at fifteen years, is rich and full-bodied, with the faintest hint of maltiness, the same malt flavour to be found in toffee or malted milk.

We should trust the judgment of whisky blenders but, as one cannot repeat too often, taste is purely subjective and so must individual preferences be. No one could deny that both Cragganmore and Longmorn are fine whiskies, but I would choose neither to take with me to my shepherd's hut. I would prefer the single malt from Linkwood, a marvellously subtle whisky, and I do not believe my judgment is influenced by the beauty of the distillery. On my last visit to Linkwood swans were swimming on its small loch in the fading summer sunshine, smoothly and with a classic majesty, symbolic of what one has come to expect of whisky from the valley of the Spey.

4

The Road to the North

For centuries the whole of the north of Scotland was inaccessible and thus virtually unknown. Life in the Highlands was feudal, the people ruled by and dependent on clan chieftains, who insisted on absolute loyalty. The bloody warfare endemic in the north was warfare between clans, which seldom united against a common enemy. Even at Culloden more than one clan fought on the side of the English against Prince Charles Edward. The massacre of Glencoe was the most shameful example of perfidy and bloodthirstiness in the Highlands, but it was not the only one.

Before the 1715 rebellion there were no roads suitable for

wheeled traffic north of the River Tay. This inaccessibility was the main reason why the government had never been able to suppress the power of the clans. When it decided that their unruliness could no longer be endured, Parliament passed laws to disarm the clans, to forbid the wearing of the kilt and to abolish the heritable jurisdiction of clan chiefs. They also decided to build roads.

General Wade was given the task of constructing them and he built a network of roads, mainly connecting the military establishments which had been set up at Fort William, Fort Augustus and Fort George. The work was shoddy and soon the surfaces began to crumble, making them almost as difficult to traverse as the old paths over the moors and through the forests, along which the whisky smugglers used to lead their caravans of pack-horses. Early in the next century it was not a soldier but an engineer, Thomas Telford, who built the roads that finally opened up the Highlands, allowing the English to begin 'colonising' Scotland by acquiring sporting estates and building their unspeakably ugly turreted mansions, which unsuspecting tourists today believe to be Scottish castles.

One of the most handsome bridges which Telford built was over the River Spey, just outside Craigellachie, which was in use until the 1970s, when the changing demands of road transport forced it into obsolescence. For some reason – it may have been topography or financial constraints – Telford had sited the bridge in such a way that its north end was approached from round a sharp bend in the road. It was still navigable, if that is the word, by the Alexander's buses, which provided the local service, but only after the drivers had learnt a trick. As they came to the bridge, they would line the front of their bus up on a series of fissures in the rock face on the right of the road and only when they reached a predetermined mark, which they all knew, would they turn the steering-wheel round sharply and the bus would swing smoothly on to the bridge. When long-distance coaches and huge continental trucks arrived with the sanction of the European Community, their drivers could only get on to the bridge by going forwards and backwards two or three times in the manner of a learner practising a three-point turn. This was too much for their patience or their vanity and a new functional and ungraceful bridge, not much more than a road over the river, had to be built. Telford's bridge, an elegant monument to his skill, still stands there, forlorn and ignored.

Another notable bridge, the Erskine Bridge, was built much more recently to span the River Clyde between Glasgow and Dumbarton. Close to it, on the north bank of the river, is Auchentoshan distillery. Although it is situated only marginally below the Highland Line, it has accepted philosophically and without resentment its designation as a Lowland malt distillery.

In contrast to the wild beauty of the Highlands, the region of Scotland south of Glasgow and Edinburgh is placid and unexciting. In the gently undulating fields and the woodlands of the Lowlands one can forget that here too there were centuries of violence, not clan wars but fierce border raids and skirmishes. Lowland malt whiskies, pleasant and equable, unlikely to stimulate either the palate or the imagination, reflect the nature of the land, not its history. Yet today, with the growing interest in single malt whisky, the small number that are on sale deserve the attention of any discerning drinker. Auchentoshan is one of them.

John Milne, whose company, Eadie Cairns, owned the distillery at the time, tells a story of how the Erskine bridge was constructed to replace a ferry which shuttled to and fro across the Clyde on chains; a journey of not much more than a couple of hundred yards, but one which saved travellers a long and tedious detour through Glasgow. On the day when it was announced that the Erskine Bridge was going to be built, John and a colleague went from the distillery to a pub just alongside the bridge. There they found Murdo Macmurdo, the skipper of the two-man crew which operated the ferry. As tactfully as he could, John asked Murdo what he felt about the fact that his ferry was to be replaced by a bridge.

'I'm nae that bothered,' Murdo replied. 'After thirty years at sea, I'm ready for a job on shore.'

Auchentoshan is one of only three malt distilleries in Scotland which uses triple distillation rather than the conventional double distillation. Benrinnes on Speyside and Rosebank near Falkirk are the other two. The Irish have tried to make advertising capital out of the fact that their whisky is distilled three times, without explaining why this should be an advantage. As a general principle, the more often one distils a liquid, whether it be a mash of cereals or grapes, the more of its flavouring constituents are removed, until ultimately one is left with neutral spirit. Donald Macinlay, a fifth-generation whisky blender, always laughs at the pretensions of the Irish. In Scotland, he says, we get a perfect spirit by distilling it twice, so why do we need a third attempt? Having said that, one must concede that both Auchentoshan and Rosebank are whiskies with a distinctive character of their own and both will stand comparison with all but the very best of Highland malts.

Some years ago I was asked to appear on a television programme with two whisky blenders, Michael Martin and Ian Brown. My role was to conduct and adjudicate in a 'nosing' contest between them. I was to provide samples of Highland, Lowland and Islay whiskies, a grain whisky and a blended Scotch, which would be poured into unmarked glasses and which they would be asked to nose and place in their correct categories. In the normal way this test was one which they would easily be able to do, but on stage and in the heat of floodlights it would not be so simple. While we were discussing the programme before the day, they asked me what samples I would be taking to the studios. When I said I had in mind to take a sample of Rosebank as the Lowland malt, they rounded on me.

'Rosebank!' they exclaimed in unison. 'No way! You find another one.'

Rosebank, they agreed, would be far too difficult to distinguish from a Highland malt in those circumstances. They were both good friends of mine and one does not make life difficult for friends. So I found another Lowland malt. On the day, they both identified the samples correctly and the studio audience must have been as impressed with their skill as I was.

Another Lowland malt of distinction comes from Pencaitland, east of Edinburgh. Glenkinchie distillery is situated in some of the most fertile farming land in Scotland. A farm adjacent to the distillery belongs to it. Now let to tenants for grazing, it was for many years farmed by the distillery manager, Willie McPherson. His cattle were outstanding and won innumerable prizes at agricultural shows, including championships at Smithfield. The by-products of distilling, used as a supplement to their feed, helped to raise them in fine condition, but one cannot help wondering whether the occasional teaspoonful of whisky may also have been slipped into the trough, to give the beasties that virile bearing which always influences judges.

Farming and distilling were inseparably tied in the early days, and it is still true. Except in the infrequent years of bad harvests when not enough is available, Scottish barley is used in the making of malt whisky. The barley must be of the right quality and match the specification laid down by the distiller. It must be low in moisture, so that it does not have to be dried, and low in nitrogen. Nitrogen displaces the fermentable starch in the barley and results in a lower fermentable extract. This requirement can cause the farmer a problem, for many fertilisers contain nitrogen. Grain size, straw strength and enzyme activity are also important if the barley is to give the highest yield.

Research funded by distillers and brewers is constantly resulting in the development of several new strains of malting barley. Farmers are usually thought to be a prosaic race, their imaginations as well as their feet firmly planted in good, tenacious soil, but surprisingly they tend to choose romantic names for their new barleys: Natasha, Pipkin, Halcyon, Golden Promise. At about the time of Prince Andrew's wedding, one new strain was christened 'Fergie' as a compliment to his bride. Not long afterwards when the Duchess of York had just given birth to a bonnie girl, a report of the Institute of Brewing commented that 'Fergie's yield was disappointing'. One likes to think that distillers could have been more tactful.

During the Second World War the government first reduced the amount of barley available for making whisky and then, in 1942, cut off all supplies to distillers. With the outcome of the Battle of the Atlantic still very much in doubt and the need to use all home grown barley as animal feed, the government's action was understandable. Today the situation and the economics are very different. In the first place, the United Kingdom now grows a substantial surplus of barley, which is exported. Equally important is the fact that a tonne of barley used to make malt whisky, with the by-products of draff and dark grains being fed to animals, will make a far larger contribution to the national economy by way of income for farmers, excise revenue and export earnings than the same quantity of barley used to feed animals or people.

Anyone who wishes to appreciate the great variety of malt whiskies that are distilled in Scotland should be prepared to travel, for many distilleries do not bottle their whisky as a single malt but supply it only to blenders. They are to be found dotted around the Highlands, and a journey to find them will not entail any hardship for much of it will be through countryside of spectacular beauty. The Erskine Bridge is as good a place as any from which to set out. Suppressing the temptation to take any road, high or low, to Loch Lomond, which must be one of the most publicised but overrated of Scotland's tourist attractions, and heading north, one will reach Glengoyne distillery by the village of Dumgoyne at the foot of the Campsie Fells.

Glengoyne is only fractionally north of the Highland Line, just as Auchentoshan is fractionally to the south of it, and to pretend that this purely geographical distinction should have any material effect on the whisky that the two produce seems absurd. This is in no way meant to denigrate Glengoyne, which is a distillery well worth visiting, small and neat and so compact that the sequence of the distilling processes are easy to follow. Moreover it is delightfully sited, in front of a narrow glen through which flows the stream from which it draws its water. The stream has been dammed and above the dam a reception centre has been built where visitors can be entertained. In spring, when the slopes of the glen are so carpeted with daffodils that even Wordsworth would have been amazed, there can be no better place to sit and take a glass of malt whisky which is light and fresh and inclined to sweetness, but none the worse for that.

No imaginary line, however skilfully drawn, can mark the separation of Scotland into Lowlands and Highlands better than nature has done. Moving north from Glengoyne one reaches Aberfoyle, a restful village below the mountains which mark the beginning of the Trossachs. To find such unspoilt beauty so close to the claustrophobic ugliness of Scotland's industrial belt seems miraculous, no matter how often one visits it. From the mountains and moors innumerable burns run down through the heather into silent, jewelled lochs bordered by forests of fir and spruce and larch, with Loch Katrine the loveliest of them all. It is as though all the variety of topography to be found in Scotland has been concentrated in a miniature panorama which will tempt the traveller into journeying further north.

Heading eastwards along the north shore of Loch Earn one will reach Crieff, at one time the most important local tryst, a centre for cattle trading. Droves of cattle would be brought from all over the Highlands, and even from the Western Isles, to be sold at Crieff. They would have been brought through the same mountain passes and along the same paths as the whisky smugglers followed with their pack-horses, bringing their whisky to the trysts. In the first half of this century Crieff had a reputation as a health resort and, like other similar Scottish towns, had a hydropathic hotel. A friend of mine remembers being taken as a small boy to spend holidays at Crieff Hydro. It was an annual expedition, the whole family travelling to Perth by train and then being driven to arrive in style at the Hydro's imposing entrance. As well as trunks, hatboxes, tennis racquets and golf clubs, their luggage always included an extra valise stout enough to hold a fortnight's supply of whisky, sherry and vintage port, with perhaps a bottle of madeira for an elderly aunt. The reason for this secret profligacy was that no alcohol was served at the Hydro, either in the dining-room or anywhere else. As a result, every evening before dinner and more often than not afterwards, guests held parties in their bedrooms, taking it in turns to invite or be invited by other friends staying at the Hydro. The management were supposed to disapprove of these Bacchanalian revels, but like all good Scots were ready to supply glasses, soda water and ice for a modest charge.

Glenturret distillery lies just outside the town, and like some others puts forward a claim to being the oldest distillery in Scotland, for some of its buildings date back to 1775. In fact the distillery became defunct in the 1920s and was only revived just over thirty years ago. James Fairlie, a local man active in politics, headed a consortium of businessmen who invested in the venture. The distillery is the second smallest in Scotland, so small that one can see all of the processes of distillation in a short walk and a matter of minutes. In spite of this, or perhaps because of it, James has cleverly made Glenturret a tourist attraction. With the help of grants from Scottish tourist organisations, he has built a visitors' centre with an audio-visual presentation, a museum and a restaurant. Now holidaymakers come to the distillery in coachloads from Crieff.

As a single malt Scotch Whisky, Glenturret is available in different bottlings and at a number of different ages. I have always found it a little bland for my personal taste, but clearly not everyone agrees with that view, for one can see it being served in the bar of the Caledonian Club in London whose members, all exiled Scots, are discriminating in their choice of whiskies and people say it is also popular in the bars of the House of Commons. Trevor Cowan, a blender whose judgment I trust, says that it improves to a surprising degree with age and that the 15-year-old Glenturret is one of the great single malts.

The distillery and its amenities are constantly being improved, and I was once invited to a lunch in the nearby Foulford Inn held by James Fairlie to celebrate the completion of one stage of its development. The principal guest at the lunch was Nicholas Fairbairn, later Sir Nicholas, at that time the Conservative MP for Perth and Kinross. The other guests, local farmers and a good sprinkling of James's distiller friends, may have been surprised to see Nicky Fairbairn wearing a white brocade waistcoat with his business suit, but they did not show it. Anyway they certainly appreciated his witty speech, during the course of which he told a story about the then Labour Chancellor of the Exchequer.

The Chancellor, it seemed, had recently spent a holiday in Kenmore, a village on Loch Tay not far from Crieff. He was staying in the village's one hotel and on the morning after his arrival he strolled across to the village shop, where he picked out some picture postcards, a film for his camera, toothpaste and one or two other odds and ends. When the shopkeeper had wrapped up his purchases, the Chancellor discovered that he had left his wallet in the hotel.

'Will it be all right,' he asked the shopkeeper, 'if I take these with me and come back to pay you later?'

The man looked at him sternly. 'That may be the way you run the country, Chancellor, but we dinna do business like that here!'

The story may only be a story but it is wholly believable. The shopkeeper's reply typifies the combination of business acumen and Presbyterian rectitude of which most Scots thoroughly approve and which only on isolated occasions slips into farce.

Not infrequently one may find James Fairlie or his son Peter, who manages the distillery, at lunchtime in the Foulford Inn, which lies on the road from Crieff to the Sma'

Glen. This is understandable for, although the inn is an unpretentious establishment, the lunches are excellent, offering all those staple Scottish dishes which are becoming hard to find and which no housewife south of the border seems capable of cooking correctly: lentil soup with sippets, mince and tatties, fillet of haddock and clootie dumplings. Mrs Beaumont and her family have resisted any temptation to experiment with nouvelle cuisine. Sensibly, for your Scottish countryman takes no pleasure in being offered a neat pattern of green fruit slices and pomegranate balls surrounding two ounces of pink lamb.

Sheena, a young lady I know who works for the Scottish Tourist Board, once found herself, when her boss was taken ill, having to escort a coachload of French and German farmers on a tour of Scotland. Only a tourist authority would put Germans and French together and as Sheena could speak neither language, communication was difficult and she was relieved when the coach pulled in for lunch at the Foulford Inn. Maureen, Mrs Beaumont's daughter-in-law, was behind the bar that day and soon the farmers were chatting happily to her. Sheena learnt then that Maureen had taken her degree at Aberdeen University in languages and that French and German had been her main subjects. Her charm, a bar lunch and a couple of drams of Glenturret single malt whisky soon dispelled all sullen suspicion and the farmers were singing each other's songs as they set out on the road to the Sma' Glen.

Although it is listed in guidebooks as a beauty spot, the Sma' Glen, a ravine between steep hills, has never struck me as exceptionally beautiful. On a sunny day, as one drops down the road towards the stream at the bottom of the glen, the sunshine disappears and one feels an uneasiness and an urge to hurry through, as though to avoid any supernatural presence that might be lurking there. Of course it is no more than superstition, but I have experienced the same uneasiness in other places in Scotland.

For exceptional beauty one need only follow the road from the Sma' Glen across the moors to Aberfeldy. At one point there is a spectacular view of the Perthshire mountains and in particular of Schiehallion, as beautifully shaped and graceful as any mountain in Scotland. The name is from the Gaelic and has been translated by some as 'Fairy Hill' and by others as 'The Maiden's Breast', descriptions which the imaginative and the poetic might feel are almost synonymous.

One of the great and best loved figures in the whisky business, Archie Watson of Charles Mackinlay and Company, had a house by Loch Rannoch at the foot of Schiehallion where he stayed at weekends and to which he eventually retired. He once invited me to stay there and when I arrived he apologised for not having a television set in the house. Schiehallion, dwarfing everything below, made it impossible to receive television pictures unless an aerial were installed at a suitable place on the peak and the price he had been quoted for doing that seemed absurd, even though he was not short of a bawbee or two, as they say. We fished the loch that afternoon and television would have only been an unwelcome intrusion on an evening spent talking, exchanging stories of the whisky business which had been his life.

Aberfeldy is a typical small Highland town with one of General Wade's better bridges, but no other great claim to fame beyond the poem 'The Birks o' Aberfeldy' which Robert Burns wrote in praise of its beautiful setting. The townsfolk may feel a touch of jealousy for the nearby village of Fortin-gall, which has been known to claim that Pontius Pilate was born in a Roman camp there, a dubious boast surely, and one wonders whether those who first made it had taken too freely of Aberfeldy malt whisky. The distillery is just beyond Aberfeldy and the whisky matches the character of the town, pleasant and comfortable, 'couthie' as they say in Scotland, without inspiring any great excitement.

From Aberfeldy, after crossing the Tay, one reaches Pitlochry, a holiday town which claims to be the geographical centre of Scotland. On its fringes are two distilleries, Blair Athol and Edradour. Blair Athol was one of the first in Scotland to build a reception centre for visitors, and this is now highly organised to a point when it almost overshadows what was a small, traditional and picturesque distillery. Without wishing to be uncharitable, one cannot help feeling that in an odd way it appears to have detracted from the reputation of Blair Athol as a single malt and one seldom hears about it.

Edradour is the smallest distillery in Scotland. Three men can run it comfortably and its stills are the smallest that Customs and Excise regulations will allow, on the basis that if they were any smaller they would be too easy to conceal. The shadows of the whisky smugglers are never far away. The distillery is well worth a visit, especially for those who are pressed for time, since you will be given a good insight into the making of malt whisky in twenty minutes or so and the chances are that you will be given a dram as well.

The distillery was built on the estate of the Duke of Atholl, head of the Clan Murray, whose home Blair Castle lies only a few miles away. Most castles to be found in Scotland are rugged and austere, suited to withstand both the aggression of rival clans and the rigours of the Scottish climate. Blair Castle, white and elegant, set in pleasant, friendly parkland, seems to belong to another world, the world of fairy princesses and knights-at-arms and troubadours.

The castle gave shelter to Prince Charles Edward on his glorious march to the south in 1745 and again on his inglorious retreat. Others might well have had their lands confiscated or even their heads forfeited for openly supporting the Jacobite cause in this way, but clearly the Dukes of Atholl were diplomats. They retained the royal favour and in the following century when Queen Victoria spent a night at the castle on her way to the north, the Duke's retainers stayed all night on guard in the grounds, watching over her safety.

Their loyalty so moved the Queen that she conferred on the Duke the right to maintain a private army, a privilege unique in Britain and one which the present Duke still enjoys. Today the Atholl Highlanders and their pipers are only a ceremonial force, but one in which any Scotsman would be honoured to enlist.

For a county which would seem to have all the attributes needed to make good malt whisky, Perthshire has relatively few distilleries. One has to travel a good way north of Pitlochry to find Dalwhinnie. The little village, which claims to be the highest in Scotland, and its distillery offer a welcome oasis after crossing the frighteningly barren moors around Drumochter pass. The inn in the village was built as a residence for General Wade, and when Queen Victoria once spent a night there, she did not receive the hospitality she had enjoyed at Blair Castle. She complained of having to dine on 'two miserable starved Highland chickens'.

The distillery at Dalwhinnie is also an official meteorological station and the manager reports daily to the central meteorological office on the prevailing temperature, air pressure and rainfall. He is paid a very modest stipend for this chore, which can be an unwelcome one in winter when the instruments are often buried beneath a foot or two of snow.

Until recently Dalwhinnie was only available as a single malt locally but it is now included in United Distillers' range of classic malts. The other day a wine merchant near my home was promoting it by offering customers a glass of 15-year-old Dalwhinnie to taste. I found it a pleasant enough dram, but would not face Drumochter pass in winter if that were the only means of drinking it. As always this is a personal view, and some of my friends in the whisky business were delighted to find that Dalwhinnie is now freely available.

Such is the current vogue for giving labels or tags to everything, that people have even begun subdividing the recognised classifications of malt distilleries. We are now told that there are Southern, Northern, Eastern and Western Highland malts. As my daughters would say, this surely is O.T.T. In the Western Highlands only three distilleries are listed, and one of these is silent at the present time. Even so, it is worth leaving the A9 at Dalwhinnie and heading for the west coast along the road to Spean Bridge. The road is not one for the impatient motorist, for much of it is single track, with passing places marked out with posts. People who drive in the Highlands for the first time may find single track roads – and there are plenty of them – irritating, for they are never sure whether they should stop or wait for the oncoming car to do so. No one of course has the right of way, but one quickly gets the hang of it and begins to enjoy the appreciative hand signal of the motorists for whom one stops. In this way single track roads serve a useful purpose, acclimatising the visitor to the leisurely pace and courtesy of the Highlands.

Narrow though it is, the road from Dalwhinnie to Spean Bridge is charming, winding its way through woodlands, with glimpses of the mountains ahead. Suddenly one sees Ben Nevis, the highest mountain in Britain and for much of the year capped with snow. People are often skiing in the area as late as May. At the foot of the mountain stands Ben Nevis distillery, founded in 1825 by John Macdonald, later known as 'Long John', a name which survives on the label of a well-known blended Scotch.

The distillery has an interesting, one might almost say bizarre, history. At one time it was owned by Joe Hobbs, a colourful character who became involved in the whisky business in the 1930s. He has been described as a Canadian or a Scot living in Canada, where he is said to have either made a fortune or lost one, or both. Whatever the truth, he appears to have found an ingenious way of assuaging the thirst of Americans in the long, dry years of Prohibition. How he did that is not known with any certainty, but one story is that he simply loaded his motor yacht with Scotch and ferried it across Lake Ontario, a perfectly plausible story, for it was only one of many ways by which Scotch was smuggled into America. When he came to Scotland, Hobbs began buying malt whisky distilleries. At one time he owned Bruichladdich on the Isle of Islay, Glenkinchie and a share in Glenury, but it was not until 1955 that he acquired Ben Nevis.

He also started an American-style cattle ranch along the Great Glen. They say that some of his ranch hands were as eccentric as himself and would go into nearby Fort William wearing the stetsons, chaps, boots and spurs of an American cowboy. One imagines that they were not allowed to carry six-shooters, but even so they must have livened up the Saturday night dances. Another of Hobbs' ventures was to buy nearby Inverlochy Castle and convert it into a luxurious and very expensive hotel, which today, together with Culloden House, Tulchan Lodge and Cromlix House in Doune, is on the 'circuit' for rich Americans touring Scotland.

Now Ben Nevis distillery is owned by the Japanese drinks

company Nikka. The acquisition of Scotland's distilleries by the Japanese – Tomatin just south of Inverness is also owned by a Japanese firm – causes the same uneasiness that was felt when North Americans began buying their way into the whisky business back in the 1930s. Today the American presence is accepted and in retrospect need not have caused any more alarm than the investment by British companies in the port wine, madeira and sherry trades during the last century.

At one time the whisky made at Ben Nevis had a very dubious reputation, but now the Japanese are carrying out a major reconstruction of the distillery and seem anxious that it should produce a malt whisky that will match the standard of other Highland malts. I visited Ben Nevis not long ago and Colin Ross, a very experienced and knowledgeable distillery manager, gave me a dram to taste. Although the whisky was well above normal bottling strength, it was in no way fiery, but smooth and mild. I could detect no trace of the sea tang which one usually finds in whiskies from distilleries situated near the coast, but it is perhaps too early to pass judgment and one should wait until the reconstruction work is finished and the whisky now being made has been allowed to mature.

A yacht named *Ocean Mist*, owned by Hobbs, was recently sold by his heirs to three Edinburgh people and sailed up the Caledonian Canal and down the east coast of Scotland to Leith, where it was to be fitted out as a floating restaurant. Getting the boat through the locks on the Caledonian Canal and again into the docks at Leith caused major problems. Recently I was in Leith and saw the yacht, now rechristened *The African Queen*, its paintwork chipped, its fittings tarnished. A notice fixed to it said it was for sale, so one presumes that the restaurant venture has been a failure. I could not help wondering whether it was the same boat in which swashbuckling Hobbs had defied the US coastguards to give Americans the whisky which a crassly stupid law was denying them. If it is, then it is sad to see a little piece of the folklore of Scotch come to an ignoble end.

Not far south of Fort William is another distillery, the whisky from which does have the authentic tang of the sea. Oban was once a prosperous Victorian town and a railway terminus, but is now just a tourist centre, providing a ferry link to both the Inner and the Outer Hebrides. Silhouetted against the skyline behind the distillery is McCaig's Folly, an extraordinary structure to find in a Highland port, modelled on the Colosseum in Rome and constructed towards the end of the last century simply to provide work for unemployed builders.

Across the sea for Oban is Mull, quickly reached by ferry. On a hill above the island's main town of Tobermory, best known for the wreck of a Spanish Armada galleon lying at the bottom of the bay in front of it, is a distillery, now also called Tobermory, although it originally was known as Ledaig. Founded as long ago as 1798, it was silent for long periods in the last century. Since it was revived in the 1970s it has been worked only intermittently and is silent again now, but the owner is confident that it will reopen as soon as the economic climate improves.

Just off the southern tip of Mull is the island of Iona where in AD 563 St Columba established a centre from which Christianity was carried into Scotland. Mention of early Christian missionaries often prompts someone to ask when it was that the Scots first began to make whisky. The answer is that no one knows. The first recorded reference to whisky is acknowledged to be in the Scottish Exchequer Rolls of 1494, which mentions 'eight bols of malt' being given to a Friar John Cor with which to make 'aquavitae'. The word whisky is derived from 'uisge beatha', which is the Gaelic for aquavite or the water of life, which was certainly being distilled in Scotland well before that time. Some writers have suggested that the art of distillation was brought to Scotland by missionary monks from Ireland, and to support this hypothesis they point out that monastic communities have always been engaged in making wine, beer and liqueurs. A contrary theory is that the Celts, who had a civilisation of their own in Europe before coming to Britain, were distilling a brew of cereals even before brandy began to be distilled from wine. All we know with any certainty is that whisky was being made in Ireland when that country was invaded by the English towards the end of the twelfth century. As there had been an interflow of people between Scotland and Ireland for centuries, it is extremely likely that whisky was also being distilled in Scotland by that time.

Irish distillers, hoping no doubt to claim a share of the international cachet that now belongs to Scotch, have made much of claims that they were making whisky before the Scots. Whether they did or not will never be known, but there is a persistent legend that it was St Patrick who brought them the secret of this wonderful elixir, the long-awaited cure for senility as it was then thought to be. If this is true, then some credit should go to Scotland, for St Patrick was himself a Scot, born in Dumbarton on the River Clyde.

Throughout summer one can see parties of middle-aged English visitors being driven in coaches through Scotland on tours which encompass all the main historical landmarks and beautiful scenery which the country has to offer. One such group was in the charge of a driver who also gave them a running commentary on whatever they were passing. Throughout the tour they passed a number of battlefields, some relatively obscure, where, the driver told his passengers with some pride, a handful of gallant Scots had destroyed a much larger and better equipped English army.

Finally they came to Bannockburn, where he could tell them without exaggeration that Robert the Bruce with 6,000 men routed an army of more than 17,000 under Edward II. A monument has been built to commemorate the victory, and having the driver draw it to his attention was too much for an Englishman at the back of the coach.

'Did we English never win a battle against the Scots?' he asked with trenchant sarcasm.

'Not as long as I'm in charge of this coach you didn't,' the driver replied firmly.

We Scots are proud of our victories and of our reputation for unmatched courage in battle. Who else but Highland Scots would have sent an infantry regiment to stop a German armoured division which was pursuing a retreating South African force, as the Black Watch did in North Africa? We can find pride, too, not shame in the defeats we have suffered. Culloden Moor, where in 1746 the ragged remnant of Prince Charles's army was massacred by the redcoats of the Duke of Cumberland with a savagery beyond belief and Scotland's aspirations for independence finally extinguished, is a national shrine.

For five months after Culloden the Prince was a fugitive, hunted by government troops, wandering through the Highlands and the Western Isles with a reward of £30,000 offered for his capture. Some of the time was spent on the Isle of Skye where Flora Macdonald earned herself a place in history by helping him. Then he returned to the mainland and when at last a French ship arrived, made a last dash for its protective safety, covering the hundred miles from Ben Alder to Arisaig within a week.

A long time later, 238 years to be exact, a group of whisky men decided to relive that final dash to freedom. The idea to retrace the Prince's journey was that of Michael Thompson of the Perth whisky firm Peter Thompson. He was accompanied on the expedition by Sandy Grant Gordon, John Grant of Glenfarclas, Hector Maclennan of Ballantines and Sandy Corstorphine of Waverley Vintners, all whisky men. Not satisfied with taking the same route as that Prince Charles had followed, Michael decided that they should try to recreate, as accurately as they could, the conditions under which the Prince had made the journey, wearing the same kind of clothes, eating the same food and sleeping rough.

So everyone in the group wore the 'Feileadh Mor' plaid, a length of tartan sixteen feet long and five feet wide, wound round the body and belted at the waist, which they used at night as a sleeping blanket. They had also intended to live off the land, each taking with him only a quantity of oatmeal and a bottle of whisky, and hoping to cook whatever they could snare or catch over a campfire at night. Prudently they cheated a little and caches of food, chickens and a haunch of venison were left for them at strategic points along their route. The chickens were alive, which gave John Grant a chance to prove his talents as a cook, but only after killing, plucking and cleaning them. They had hoped to relieve the monotony of their diet, overloaded with oatmeal, with fish from the lochs they passed, but caught only four small ones. Heavy rain forced them to spend some nights in mountain bothies, but they succeeded in finishing the trek, footsore but with no cases of terminal exhaustion and a new respect for Prince Charles Edward.

The old Scottish song has it that the road to the isles is 'by Loch Tummel and Loch Rannoch and Loch Aber', but today the conventional route to the Isle of Skye is by road or rail to

Kyle of Lochalsh, before crossing the Sound of Sleat by the ferry which operates a service every few minutes through the day. Kyleakin, where the ferry lands, with its drab cafés and souvenir shops, offers a depressing introduction to Skye, and a more attractive though longer journey is by the alternative ferry from Mallaig on the mainland to Armadale in Sleat.

No other island of the Hebrides can match Skye in beauty or in the contrast of its scenery; a range of jagged peaks thrusting into the sky, a bewildering coastline indented with fiords and sea lochs, spectacular cliffs, lonely moors, green fields bordered with white cottages, all in an ever-changing light of extraordinary clarity. In the nineteenth century the Cuillins attracted mountaineers from all over Europe to climb their peaks, while Victorian ladies would try to emulate Turner by painting or sketching them. The island's name in Gaelic – Eileen a' Cheo – means 'the misty isle' and could scarcely be more appropriate. One can spend days there, even weeks, and never see the tops of the Cuillins. Only on my third visit did I see them for the first time and then unexpectedly, rounding a bend as I drove from Portree to Sligachan. The sensation was unbelievable, almost frightening. Suddenly the valley through which I had passed a dozen times was transformed, hemmed in with mountains which dominated it with their claustrophobic grandeur.

Turn inland at Sligachan and the road will take you to Loch Harport, one of the island's many sea lochs. On the edge of the loch, in the shadow of the Cuillins, you will find Talisker distillery. When it was built in 1830 a local minister, the Reverend Roderick Macleod, felt that its construction would be 'one of the greatest curses that, in the ordinary course of providence, could befall it or any other place'. In the event, although comparatively few people are needed to run a distillery, Talisker has provided continuity of employment on an island where the population has been progressively shrinking for more than a hundred years and which today can offer few worthwhile prospects for its young people.

Once when I was on Skye collecting background material for a novel, I dropped in at the police station in Portree. It was a Sunday afternoon, and the Free Church of Scotland makes sure that nothing happens in Skye on Sunday. Even the swimming pool is not allowed to be used, so the young police sergeant was glad of an opportunity to make conversation. He was from Aberdeen and told me at length about the short-comings of the people of Skye, their laziness, their super-stitions, their suspicion of incomers. Then, after forty minutes of invective, he smiled. 'Ah!' he said, 'but it's a grand place to stay!'

Incomers, reluctant though they may be to admit it, usually fall in love with Skye. As someone once said, it is not an island, it is an intoxication. One incomer who did was Derek Bottomer, the manager of Talisker distillery until recently when his company posted him back to the mainland. He once told me that he and his wife had been walking the hills for eleven wonderful hours on the previous Saturday. He was also an enthusiastic member of the Mountain Rescue Team. Beautiful though they may be, the Cuillins can also be treach-erous. In any one year the members of the Mountain Rescue Team will be called out several times, more often than not at night, to risk their own lives bringing down visitors who have gone climbing, either not properly equipped or ignoring the rules of safety.

Talisker is a fine malt whisky. The peatiness is there and so is the tang of the sea, but in flavour it is far more delicate than say, Lagavulin, the Islay distillery which belongs to the same company. On my first visit to Skye I tried to interest Derek in my theory about the island peat being drenched in sea spray and passing its flavour on through the malt. He listened to me courteously and then explained as kindly as he could that the malted barley used at Talisker comes from the mainland. So, as always, we are back to water.

On that same visit I was staying at the Skeabost House Hotel and after returning there from Talisker, still not wholly ready to condemn my theory about island whiskies to oblivion, that evening I tried a small experiment in the bar. Lining up glasses of island malt whiskies, Talisker, of course, and Lagavulin and Highland Park from Orkney, I nosed them in turn like a blender would, shaking the glasses first gently to release the aroma of the whiskies and looking for similarities between them as well as for differences in character.

A man not far along the bar was watching me curiously and, I suspected, with amusement. So I explained to him what I was doing.

'Aye,' he said, 'there is a likeness in the three of those whiskies surely. Think of them as musical instruments all playing a similar tune. Lagavulin is the double bass, Highland Park has the seductive murmur of a cello. As for Talisker, it's more sophisticated; a French horn, would you say, even an oboe?'

Naturally I assumed he must be in the whisky business, not working at Talisker, for we were some distance from the distillery, but perhaps a visitor from a distillery on the mainland. But no, he was from a garage in Portree and also owned a croft not far from Kingsburgh where Prince Charles spent one night sheltering from the pursuing troops.

On Skye one cannot escape Bonnie Prince Charlie, for everywhere on the island there are reminders and legends of him; the grave of Flora Macdonald who helped him to escape, the hotel in Portree where they met for the last time, caves where he is supposed to have hidden. This is not history but folklore, useful for entertaining tourists.

Bonnie Prince Charlie's escapade was no more than a blip in the heart scan of Skye's history. For centuries the feud between two clans, the Macleods and the Macdonalds, affected the lives of almost everyone on the island. The history of the Macdonalds is impressively portrayed in the clan centre they have built at Sleat. Dunvegan Castle in the north-west of the island is the home of the Macleods and probably the only house in Scotland to have been inhabited by the same family for more than seven hundred years. The stories of their savage and bloody feuding are evidence of a cruelty which always seems to be not too far below the surface of life on Skye.

Linked to the cruelty, and the two may be connected, is superstition. There are still folk on Skye who believe in the sithes, the little people, who live in fairy caves, weave fairy cloth and sing fairy songs. Fairy Bridge on the road from Edinbane to Portree still arouses a tremor of fear and when horses cross it they shy and neigh. At Dunvegan Castle one may see hanging on a wall the Fairy Flag. Various stories have been told of how it came into the possession of the Macleods, but they believe – and so do others – that if it is waved when the clan is in trouble, for example in battle, it will bring powerful help from forces not of this world.

A third family, the Mackinnons, live on Skye and local people say that they have cleverly survived and taken advantage of the feud between the Macdonalds and the Macleods. They have a reputation of being skilful at flattering the ladies and at other related accomplishments. A story illustrating this concerns two Englishmen who were foolish enough to take their wives to Skye in a small, open car. Inevitably, as they were driving through the most desolate and exposed part of the island, the clouds opened to unleash a monsoon's rain.

Seeing an isolated croft, the driver stopped the car and went to knock on the door of the cottage.

'Can you help us?' he asked the man who opened it. 'Do you have a mackintosh to cover two ladies?'

The man thought for a while. 'No,' he replied at last, 'but we have a Mackinnon who has a great reputation in those matters.'

Crofting is a part of life on Skye. The population of the island is not much more than eight thousand people and yet there are some two thousand crofts. Only about one-third of them are farmed full time. Today crofters are also shop-keepers, local government officials, veterinary surgeons or carpenters. Farming an acre of so of land with a few head of cattle to graze on the common land of the township is not a viable proposition, even with the help that crofters now receive from the European Community's lunatic agricultural policy, but the determination of the island folk to preserve what they believe to be their right is intensified by the memory of what happened two hundred years ago. There can have been few injustices more cruel and more shameful than the infamous clearances. Because landowners could make more money out of the land by grazing sheep on it, whole communities, three generations or more of families, were evicted by force or by persuasion, heaped on to ships with their scanty bundles of personal possessions and sent despairingly to find an existence in lands which were not more than names to them. Even now, reading contemporary accounts of the clearances must surely arouse in all but the most hard-hearted a spurt of rage at this example of man's inhumanity to man.

The clearances have left a permanent scar on the Western Isles and the Western Highlands of Scotland. The perceptive visitor to Skye will find, beneath the beauty and romance of the island, a sadness in the people, a sadness that is reflected in their faces and even more in their haunting songs. It is the sadness of those who for more than a hundred years saw their kinsfolk driven into exile and have lived in the constant expectation that they too might be banished from their homes.

Loch Maree is the most beautiful stretch of inland water in the British Isles, lovelier than either Loch Lomond or Lake Windermere. Leaving Skye one can reach it along twisting, alpine roads over Applecross peninsula and past Loch Torridon with its spectacular backcloth of mountains, Beinn Eighe with its seven peaks running along a seven-mile ridge, Liathach and the lovely jewelled mountain, Beinn Alligin. If you stop on the road at a suitable point and look backwards to the west, you may be fortunate enough to be rewarded with one of the most breathtaking views to be had anywhere in Britain, the sun setting on Skye, dropping down over the Cuillins to extinguish its brilliance in the Atlantic.

Beautiful though it is, Wester Ross has no distilleries, and one wonders whether this might be because the water coming down from those rugged mountains is not suitable for distilling good whisky. A geologist would no doubt have the answer. Leaving the mountains behind, one eventually reaches Dingwall, a meeting place for councils in Viking days, but now an unpretentious, quiet town, so quiet that one is surprised to learn that it has associations with two men who achieved notoriety, though neither deserved it: Macbeth, in his time a humane and good king, unfairly vilified by Shakespeare, and Sir Hector MacDonald.

Macdonald achieved the feat, virtually impossible in the last century, of rising through the ranks of the British army to become a general. The hero of the Battle of Omdurman, in

1903 he was found dead of a revolver wound in a Paris hotel, shortly before he was due to be courtmartialled in Ceylon on charges of homosexual offences. Claims that he had been the victim of a conspiracy by the government of Ceylon or his fellow officers, led to an upsurge of sympathy for him. He was denied a public funeral with military honours, but a grandiose monument to him stands on a hill overlooking Dingwall. Even today the *cause célèbre* arouses passions, and a lady I recently met in the town's public library had tears in her eyes when we talked about him.

Not far from Dingwall is Muir of Ord distillery, which when it was established in 1838 was one of a group worked by a co-operative of farmers and which sold its whisky all over Wester Ross and even as far as Skye. Not long ago one passed the distillery if one drove along the A9 road, but now it has in effect been by-passed by the new bridge over the Cromarty Firth. One could not in any case have seen the distillery from the road, for it is concealed by a large, unsightly drum maltings built in 1968.

In a drum maltings the barley, after steeping, is filled into drums which by rotating carry out the same function as the maltmen who turn the barley on floor maltings. To be economic, a drum maltings must have the capacity to supply the malt requirements of six or seven distilleries situated not too far away. The whisky distilled at Muir of Ord has been mainly used in blending and particularly in the well-known White Label brand of John Dewar and Sons, but it is also bottled at twelve years as a single malt under the name Glen Ordie.

By travelling to the north through the Western Highlands one misses all the distilleries in the eastern half of Scotland. There are a dozen between Dundee and Elgin, and one might suggest without being disparaging that aspiring connoisseurs of malt whisky need not grieve too much if they are unable to visit them. This does not imply that their whisky is in any sense inferior, but with one or two exceptions they have either not produced a bottled single malt or, if they have, it does not have an outstanding reputation. One of the exceptions is Glendronach in Aberdeenshire, which is one of the few remaining distilleries to have a floor maltings. Glendronach single malt is rich in flavour, with a malty sweetness, and I always feel that one can detect a hint of its character in the blended whisky Highland Cream, a brand belonging to the Glasgow firm of William Teacher and Sons, who own the distillery.

The other distillery in the east which deserves mention is Royal Lochnagar, and not only for its royal connections. It stands not far from Balmoral Castle, and Queen Victoria visited it together with Prince Albert in 1848. They tasted the whisky and evidently liked it, for not long afterwards the distillery was rewarded with the Royal Warrant of Appointment as a supplier to the Queen.

Almost a hundred and thirty years later Lochnagar distillery was involved, though only indirectly, in another royal occasion at the centenary celebrations of the Malt Distillers' Association of Scotland. The Duke of Edinburgh accepted an invitation to be the principal guest at a banquet in Aviemore. George Grant, then chairman of the Association and the host for this splendid occasion, wore his kilt, and the Prince, also in his kilt, made a spectacular arrival in a helicopter which he was piloting himself. During the course of his speech after dinner, after paying all the right compliments to the Scotch Whisky trade for its outstanding export achievements, Prince Phillip could not resist making a reference to the distillery, which, he said, was polluting the river outside his 'holiday cottage'. Having heard his remark, I am certain in my own mind that it was meant to be lighthearted if not actually flippant. Sir Alex Macdonald, chairman of the Distillers Company, which owned the distillery, and the other principal guest, made a suitably amusing response, but he must have taken the accusation against his company seriously, for next morning almost at first light two senior directors of the company were sent to Lochnagar to make sure there was no truth in the Prince's remark. Shortly afterwards the company stopped using the prefix 'royal' before the name of the distillery. People have suggested that the decision to do so was taken by Sir Alex in a moment of pique. I knew him, and I cannot believe that this was the reason, for Sir Alex, a lawyer as well as an accountant by training, was too clever and too big a man to take offence over trifles.

Whatever the truth, the royal prefix has now been restored and no one can say it is not deserved. As a single malt Lochnagar is full-bodied and rich. I have no doubt that those who fish the River Dee alongside the distillery find as much enjoyment in a flask of it as they would from any whisky distilled on the banks of the Spey.

Returning to Muir of Ord, after any diversion to the east, and heading north, one reaches Dalmore distillery on the edge of the Cromarty Firth by Alness. To me, Dalmore and its single malt whisky seem to belong to another, more leisurely and more gracious age. This may be because both the distillery and the Glasgow firm of Whyte and Mackay to which it now belongs are associated with two whisky men, both of whom matched that description. Hartley Whyte was a tiny, gentle man, incapable one would have said of anger or malice and with a passion for motor racing, but the sporting, amateur racing of days well before Fangio, which found expression in his fine collection of vintage cars.

It was in 1960 that Whyte and Mackay merged with the

Dalmore distillery which for almost a hundred years had been owned and run by a local family, the Mackenzies. Major H.A.C. Mackenzie, grandson of the man who had bought the distillery in 1867, was managing it at the time of the merger. 'Hac' Mackenzie, as he was universally known, played an important part in the affairs of the malt whisky business and was for a time chairman of the Malt Distillers' Association. Somehow his old-world virtues, a forthright, no-nonsense robust manner coupled with an unsophisticated charm that was difficult to resist, seemed to have been absorbed into Dalmore malt whisky, or perhaps the reverse was true.

A little further up the coast outside the small town of Tain, Glenmorangie is a distillery which has a special virtue of its own, that of inspiring remarkable loyalty among those who work there. Ian McGregor, manager of the distillery until he recently retired after forty-seven years with the company, followed his father A.C. McGregor, who retired from the Board of Macdonald & Muir, the owners of the Glen-morangie, at the age of eighty-seven. When I last visited the distillery two years ago I was introduced to Alice Ross, who was living in a cottage just opposite the cooperage where her father had lived. He had been head cooper at Glenmorangie, having worked there for an almost unbelievable seventy years. As Alice was at the time nearer ninety than eighty, between them they must have seen literally millions of gallons of Glenmorangie malt whisky poured into the casks which he and his coopers had rebuilt or repaired at the distillery.

Acting was one of Ian McGregor's talents and he was a leading member of Tain Amateur Dramatic Society. People say that the only role they would not allow him to perform was one in a Chekov play in which he would have had to praise the qualities of vodka. Dramatic licence cannot be stretched as far as that!

One learns two important lessons when visiting Glenmorangie and the first is how to pronounce the name. Think of orange, they told me when I asked, and forget any notions you may have of associations with a species of ape. I find now I cannot resist correcting anyone who pronounces it incorrectly and must have irritated scores of barmen, waiters, golfers and friends, people of otherwise irreproachable virtue, by pointing out their mistake. The second lesson is more fundamental and can be something of a culture shock to anyone who might have begun to believe that they have grasped the essentials of distilling good malt whisky.

'Soft water, flowing through peat? Not at all!' I was told on my first visit. 'Our water from springs on Tarlogie Hill, just half a mile away, is hard. We believe it makes a better whisky.'

Whether Glenmorangie is better than other single malt whiskies is of course a matter of personal taste, but it is certainly different. One reason may well be the water, and another the shape of the pot stills, which are slim and tall – the tallest in Scotland, they claim. Another reason may be the fact that the company does not use sherry casks to mature the single malt, but only American oak casks which have previously been used to mature bourbon whiskey. Using sherry casks, they believe, adds not only colour but a sweetness to the whisky. Glenmorangie is very pale in colour and also very dry and crisp, with a delightful almost flowery fragrance, which makes it an ideal single malt to drink as an aperitif.

Still following the road to the north from Tain, one passes close to Dunrobin Castle, the picturebook home of the Dukes of Sutherland who, in the nineteenth century, earned notoriety for their pitiless evicting of crofters. Beyond it, Brora has a personality very different from other small Highland towns. Its people must be enterprising, for at one time or another they have had a coalmine, a saltworks, a brickworks and a spinning mill, without mentioning its distillery. Like the characters in Robert Louis Stevenson's story of Dr Jekyll and Mr Hyde, the distillery changes its name from time to time, if not its personality. It was built as Clynelish distillery in 1819 by the Marquess of Stafford, who later became Duke of Sutherland, and the spent grains from distilling were used to feed inmates of a piggery on an adjoining farm, which in their turn produced manure which is said to have greatly improved the land on which was grown the cereals needed to make the whisky.

The benefits of this primitive ecological cycle, added to the fact that it could use local coal to heat its stills, helped Clynelish to survive the next hundred and fifty years, even though many other distilleries in the Highlands foundered during times of recession in the whisky trade. In 1967, however, a new distillery was built on an adjacent site and this was given the name Clynelish, while the existing distillery was rechristened Brora. On some maps both distilleries are marked, but they no longer make whisky at Brora, although its buildings have been 'listed' as subject to a preservation order and cannot be dismantled.

Like all distilleries built in recent years, Clynelish is well planned, handsome and spacious, very different from those distilleries which have stood on the same site for a hundred years or more and where expansion has unavoidably meant an untidy juxtaposition of old and new. On a visit to the distillery in 1991 I was given a dram of its single malt, which previously I had tasted only in blenders' sample rooms, and rarely at that. It is not generally available, but I was told that the United Distillers Group who own the distillery now bottle some for sale locally. I found the whisky quite unlike any other single malt I know, and most attractive. The distinctive flavour is almost impossible to describe. One whisky writer has said it reminds him of acorns, but perhaps his thoughts were straying, making a Freudian association with the pigs grubbing not too far away. I prefer to withhold my judgment until I can nose and taste it again. This may mean another journey to the northern Highlands, but that would be no penance, for the folk of Brora are friendly and the golf course well worth another visit.

North of Brora one soon runs out of land, but fortunately not out of distilleries, for a short way across the sea in Orkney there are two. The islands offer a constant reminder of Scotland's affinity with the Vikings and were colonised and ruled by Norsemen for more than five hundred years. They were returned to Scotland in bizarre circumstances. On the marriage of his daughter Margaret to James III, King Christian of Denmark pawned the Orkney and Shetland islands to the Scottish crown in lieu of a dowry. The pledge was never redeemed, and the islands became a part of Scotland. Orkney also offers a reminder of a civilisation older even than Scotch whisky. At Skara Brae archaeologists have unearthed a wonderfully preserved neolithic village which dates back four thousand years.

Scapa distillery stands not far from Scapa Flow where the defeated German fleet scuttled itself after the First World War. The whisky distilled at Scapa has the unmistakable island flavour, even though no peat is used in its malt, a final incontrovertible proof that my theory about sea-washed peat was wrong. The tang of the sea in its flavour can only come from the water, which on the island is very peaty. Scapa is a heavy malt, some think of it as oily, and a perfectly acceptable dram, but one cannot imagine that the German sailors would have scuttled their ships only as an excuse for getting ashore so that they could drink it.

Highland Park, the other distillery in Orkney, has a history of its own, for it was built on the site of a church where the minister, Magnus Eunson, was able to offer his congregation not only spiritual comfort but a dram of the whisky he distilled himself and kept concealed under the pulpit from which he preached. Highland Park is a splendid whisky, an authentic island malt with an opulence of flavour which matches the opulence of its distinctive bottle and packaging. As the present vogue for single malt whiskies spreads, it seems certain that Highland Park must find a place among the market leaders.

In addition to whisky the Orcadians, as the islanders like to call themselves, make cheese. I visited a small cheese factory there and was disappointed to find it making not only Orkney cheese but Cheddar, Leicester, Gloucester, Wensleydale and others, all for a well-known supplier of mass-produced cheeses. Fortunately this kind of commercial deception has no parallel in the Scotch Whisky business. By legal definition Scotch Whisky is whisky made in Scotland and nowhere else, and if a bottle of Scotch is labelled as an Islay whisky one can be sure the whisky was distilled on the island of Islay, not on Skye or in Aberdeenshire. We Scots have fought very hard around the world to preserve this *appellation controlée* for our whisky, and long may we continue to defend it.

5

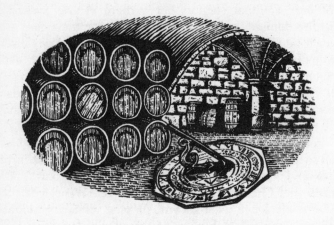

A Matter of Time

As we sat outside the Fiddichside Inn one evening in 1991, Sandy Curle and I were talking of time. This is a fine place to take a dram at any time and spring had come early, giving a warm evening sunshine to pick out the colours of the red and white tables and chairs outside the inn and the red flowers in the neat garden that slopes down to the river. The Fiddich itself gurgled over its stony bed, hurrying as though eager to become a part of the mighty whisky river which waited for it beyond the bridge over the lane.

Time may seem an odd subject for Sandy and me to be discussing, for even though whisky folk in the Spey valley do not have the same cavalier disregard for time as those in the Western Isles, it does not rank high on their list of priorities. Paradoxically this may not be because it is unimportant to them. The revers is true. Time dominates their working lives, but they have learnt that it cannot be hastened.

Time is an integral, a fundamental, part of Scotch Whisky; the thousands of years that it has taken for peat to be formed, the long springs and summers when seed sprouts and barley slowly ripens, the long hours when it germinates again in the maltings, the slow, unhurried process of mashing, fermenting and distilling. But most of all the time that is needed for spirit to become whisky.

Scotch Whisky is not entitled to that name until it has been matured in casks made of oak for at least three years. That simple statement, part of the definition of Scotch, enshrined in the country's laws, conceals a complex issue and a process which is imperfectly understood, as all but the most brash and self-opinionated will concede.

Why oak? Why three years? And how does maturation transform spirit into whisky? These are all questions which people ask, and the first is reasonably straightforward to answer. The casks must be made of wood because wood is permeable, allowing a slow process of evaporation, which is an essential part of the maturation process, and oak has proved to be the most suitable wood. Moreover, only casks made of Spanish or American oak are used, mainly because oak grown in other countries is too porous.

For many years virtually all the whisky distilled in Scotland was matured in casks that had previously held sherry. New spirit straight off the still is colourless and it takes its colour from the casks in which it is allowed to mature. Sherry casks will add an extra touch of gold to the colour and perhaps a touch of sweetness, depending on how often the cask has been used. Using sherry casks at one time had economic advantages. Sherry was an extremely popular drink in Britain, which was by far the largest export market for the shippers in Jerez. It was generally shipped to Britain in casks for bottling there. The casks once emptied were then available to the whisky trade at an attractive price, for it would have been too costly to ship them back to Spain for re-use.

This situation began to change after the Second World War for two reasons. First, the worldwide demand for Scotch increased so much and so rapidly that there were simply not enough sherry casks available to meet the whisky trade's needs. A second factor was a growing trend for the Spaniards to ship sherry in bottle rather than in cask, a trend welcomed by the Spanish government, for the manufacture of bottles and packaging material and the bottling itself would provide employment in Spain.

So the Scots had to look around for another source of casks, and they found it in the United States. Under American law a cask may only be used once to mature bourbon whiskey. American distillers find this stipulation irksome and have lobbied to have it changed, but without success. I once asked an American distiller why this should be so, and he replied sourly, 'Because the timber lobby is more powerful than the bourbon lobby.'

Whatever the reason, American oak casks, broken down into staves for shipment and reassembled in Scottish cooperages, now make up a large proportion of the 'wood', as it is called in the trade, used by the distillers of Scotland. Some people in the trade argue that American oak is in fact better than sherry wood, for whisky matured in it is lighter in colour and less sweet, and for this reason more suited to what they see as changing public taste. One cannot help wondering whether this may only be making a virtue out of necessity.

Sandy Curle would probably agree with that thought, although he might well be too courteous to voice it. For many years he was a director of Macallan distillery and at Macallan it is the company's practice to mature the whisky it intends to market as a single malt only in sherry wood. Moreover, so particular are the company and so determined to maintain the flavour and character of Macallan unchanged, that they will only use casks which have previously been used for oloroso sherry. Casks used for fino or amontillado or other types of sherry are not regarded as acceptable.

So until he retired from business, Sandy would travel to Jerez every year to select the casks he wanted. It is not enough simply for the casks to have held the right type of sherry, they must be well made and the wood sound enough to hold the whisky for twelve or eighteen years or even more, without excessive evaporation or leakage. In the course of his trips to Spain, Sandy grew to like the Spaniards and they grew fond of him. He would be asked to give talks about Scotch, explaining not only its merits as a drink, but how it was made and the part that Spain played, if only indirectly, in its production. Before long he was invited to appear on television and, dressed in his kilt, would give demonstrations of how to identify and appreciate the great varieties of Scotch. Achieving consistency in flavour and character, he believes, should be a major priority for the distiller.

'The whole art of distilling,' he told me that day at the Fiddichside Inn, 'is to make a whisky which remains consistent, day in day out, and which does not change. The whisky drinker who buys a bottle of Macallan has a right to expect this, so that has always been our aim. And so, to keep consistency, we always use the same type of casks for maturation.'

New spirit coming straight from the still at a distillery is, as anyone who has tasted it will surely agree, fiery, crude and unpalatable. Filled into an oak cask and left to mature, it is gradually transformed into a smooth, mellow spirit. To me the metamorphosis is astonishing, one of nature's miracles. Friends on the production side of the whisky business have tried patiently to explain the scientific reasons for the change. Oxidisation is a part of the process, they tell me, slowly modifying the undesirable constituents in the spirit and removing any fiery harshness. Papers on the subject have been written for scientific journals, but they do not appear to reflect any consensus in the explanations they put forward. Some years ago in a popular scientific magazine the author of an article was honest enough to admit that there are aspects of the maturation of whisky which no one yet understands. The whisky drinker might well be satisfied with that, for he does not really need to understand the scientific reasons for a phenomenon which his nose and his palate will readily accept.

The legal definition of Scotch Whisky, for both single and unblended whiskies and blends, stipulates that it must be matured for at least three years. This is no more than a minimum and the great majority of Scotch whiskies will be matured for longer than that, perhaps four or five years for blends, twelve years for most premium or de luxe blends and seven, ten, twelve, fifteen, eighteen years or even longer for single malt whiskies. What the best age is for any particular whisky must remain a matter of opinion and personal preference.

Once I was present when the head blender of a major whisky company, a blunt and honest man, was talking about Scotch to a group of Danish wine writers who were touring distilleries in Scotland. In the course of his talk he expressed his view that although whisky certainly did improve in cask, it did not do so indefinitely. After fifteen years, he claimed, there can be no further improvement and if the whisky is left in cask it will only deteriorate. He had left himself wide open for an awkward question and one of the Danes adroitly took the opening. Journalists are like that.

'If that is true, sir,' he asked, 'then how is it that your company markets a 21-year-old blend?'

The blender never flinched. As I have said, he was an honest fellow. 'That's just a marketing gimmick,' he replied.

The poor fellow may have been too honest on that occasion, for I heard not long afterwards that he was no longer with that company.

How long a whisky should be left to mature depends on a number of factors; the size and type of cask into which it is filled, the quality of the cask and the number of times it has previously been used, the kind of warehouse in which it is left to mature and, most important of all, the kind of whisky that the distiller or the blender wishes to produce and sell. Ultimately, when all these factors have been taken into account, it must be a commercial decision, for maturation is a costly process.

Apart from the expense of keeping money, in the form of whisky stocks, tied up for so long, there is the loss of whisky through evaporation. On average about 2 per cent of the whisky will evaporate each year, which means that for a 12-year-old Scotch one-quarter of the whisky will simply disappear. The French, who mature their brandy, though not generally for as long as Scotch is matured, make light-hearted remarks about the loss through evaporation being 'the angels' share', but we Scots find it hard to be flippant about expense, however necessary.

Most Scotch is matured in one of three sizes of cask; butts which hold approximately 500 litres, hogsheads which have about half that capacity and American barrels which hold between roughly 170 and 190 litres. As a general rule whisky will mature more quickly in a smaller cask. Some years ago my father-in-law, having heard that this could be done, decided that he would like to have some malt whisky distilled and bottled with his own label. It was a quixotic whim, especially as he scarcely ever drank whisky, belonging to a generation which, at an early age, had been corrupted by that singularly nasty drink which came in with flappers and the Charleston but unfortunately did not go out with them, the dry martini.

The whim also put me to a great deal of trouble. Anything is possible if you have friends in the whisky business and George Grant very kindly agreed to fill a quarter cask of Glenfarclas and to keep it at his distillery to mature. At one time a large number of private individuals used to have small casks filled for them in this way, but I believe it is unusual now. After seven years in this small cask, the whisky was ready to be bottled. Bottling so small a quantity of whisky is scarcely an economic proposition for a large modern bottling hall, and once again I had to rely on friends. Ian Brown, who had appeared in the television blending contest with me, arranged for the Glenfarclas to be put in bottles of an unusual but very attractive shape, and also for the printer who produced his company's labels to print one carrying a legend to the effect that this Glenfarclas had been specially distilled, matured and bottled for my father-in-law. At the time of ordering, the whisky had cost surprisingly little and the rent which George charged for maturing it in his warehouses was minuscule. But in the seven years since the cask was filled, the Excise Duty on whisky, already ridiculously high, had more than doubled. One good thing came out of the whole affair. My father-in-law was so shocked when the bill arrived that he forgot about martinis and settled his nerves with an outsize dram of Scotch.

In the late 1960s and the 1970s a number of private individuals, mainly in the United States, were tempted to invest in stocks of Scotch Whisky. They bought large quantities of different 'makes' of new whisky which would be held for them at the distilleries, in the belief that when the whisky was mature it would be eagerly snapped up by the blending companies, who would pay prices far in excess of what the investor had paid. Firms of so-called whisky brokers were making the transactions – taking their commission, of course – and companies were even formed with offices in New York and suitably Scottish sounding names simply for the purpose of promoting and arranging this form of 'investment'. The brochures printed by these mushroom firms gave investors the impression that all the major whisky blending companies bought matured whisky as and when they required it through brokers, rather than finding the cash to finance their own stocks.

This is simply not true. As part of their normal routine business, blending companies lay down sufficient 'fillings' of new whisky to cover what they forecast they will need so many years ahead. These stocks are financed either out of their own resources or by borrowings from banks and finance companies. No blending company of any size would rely on being able to buy the whiskies they needed either from private investors or from other sources when the time came to blend and bottle their brands.

Even so, the genuine broker does play a legitimate part in the whisky trade. When a blending company finds it is short of a certain whisky needed for its blend, it can go to a broker who may well know where that whisky can be obtained. Similarly, a broker may be useful in helping to dispose of any surplus stocks of a make of whisky or whiskies.

Private investors who were unwise enough to speculate in whisky stocks – one might call them whisky 'futures', except that there is no futures market in whisky – almost always found that when they wished to realise their investments, the whisky could only be sold, if at all, at knock-down prices. Only too often they finished by making no profit on their transactions or even losing money. Often these speculators would end up by having to rely on established brokers to sell their investments for them. The difficulty here was that by buying new whisky fillings they were in effect creating a pool of whisky – more often than not grain whisky – that nobody wanted.

Some disgruntled speculators would even complain to the Scotch Whisky Association, implying in some way that it was the fault of the Association for not warning them against such speculation, even though they had not sought its advice before parting with their money. I know of one American who, after complaining, returned home and then sent the Association a colour photograph of himself, his wife and their two teenage children, whom he had planned to put through college on the profits of his investment. On the back of the photograph he had written, 'You may like to have this reminder of two young people whose future you have ruined!'

At the Fiddichside Inn that evening Sandy told me of a new warehouse which Macallan distillers were constructing. At one time one could see at every distillery the long, low buildings in which casks of whisky were left to mature. The casks would be stacked on top of each other, two or three high, in rows which, as one went into the warehouse, one could see stretching back into the darkness. On the end of each cask would be stencilled the name of the distillery, the year in which the whisky had been distilled and the cask number. The name of the company for whom the cask had been filled might also be given on the end, or this might be shown by colour coding. At regular intervals every cask would be inspected to make sure that it had not sprung a leak.

These traditional warehouses have earth floors and are cool and damp. The temperature and humidity in them will have an effect on both the amount of whisky which is lost through evaporation and the time it takes for it to mature. Warehouses of this type still exist at many distilleries, but over the past three decades, in order to keep pace with the growth in production, more modern warehouses have been built which are larger and taller and in which the casks are stored in racks. The racking may allow for ten or even twelve casks to be stacked above each other, but the casks can more easily be handled. In the old warehouses they were rolled along the ground and lifted into place. In modern warehouses they can be speedily lifted into place or removed using special fork-lifting gear.

It had often struck me that, because in these modern warehouses the roofs are so high, the air temperature near the top must be higher than it is at ground level and that this too must affect the speed at which the whisky matures. I had never been curious enough to find out whether this was true, but now, as we were talking about maturation, I asked Sandy.

'Of course, you're right,' he replied. 'It makes a tremendous difference. That is why we have built this new warehouse at Macallan. Let's go up to the distillery and I'll show it to you.'

The new warehouse was immense; a green giant so huge that it would have seemed a monstrosity had it not been cleverly landscaped into a hillside. Sandy told me how many millions of litres of maturing whisky it would eventually be able to hold, but my mind refused to record the information. Figures of such magnitude mean nothing, not to me anyway, and all I can say is that it sounded like an awful lot of whisky.

The novelty of the warehouse is not its size, however, but its design. It is insulated and air conditioned so that not only is the temperature under the roof the same as it is at floor level, but both temperature and humidity are constant, remaining, whatever the weather conditions, at the levels which experience has shown to be ideal for the whisky distilled at Macallan.

Huge though it is, Macallan's new warehouse is dwarfed in overall size and capacity by some of the warehousing facilities built by other Scotch Whisky companies. The Glenlivet Distillers Group have what appear to be fields full of warehouses just outside Keith, but even larger are the warehouse complexes of the United Distillers Group at Blackgrange and Menstrie in Clackmannanshire. The size of these complexes with hundreds of acres of warehouses set out in geometrical uniformity 'blows the mind' as young people in Edinburgh might say. Touring just the exteriors of the warehouses involves a car journey of several minutes. The value of the whisky that lies in the warehouses is incalculable, making even the fortunes of Arab sheiks seem trivial. Other distillers, with perhaps just a touch of envy, have christened the complexes 'Fort Knox'.

Much of the whisky which lies maturing in these complexes is grain whisky, distilled in patent still distilleries in the central belt of Scotland. Grain whisky is a subject which must be approached with delicacy. Whisky people are reluctant to talk about it and, when they do, it is in the manner of a grand lady mentioning a poor relation, kindly but with condescension, implying that she is a person of no consequence. As a result of this, the important role which grain whisky plays in blended Scotch has passed largely unnoticed.

The name grain whisky is in any case a misnomer. All whisky is made from cereals, in other words grain. Two types of whisky are distilled in Scotland and the principal difference between them is in the way they are distilled. It would be more logical and more meaningful to talk of them as pot still whisky and patent still whisky, but it is now too late to change and any attempt to do so would probably cause more confusion. The other difference is that pot still whisky is made only from malted barley and can therefore be called malt whisky, while patent still whisky is made from a relatively small proportion of malted barley, together with other unmalted cereals, usually maize or wheat.

This may sound straightforward enough and people may well wonder what it is about grain whisky which provokes this reticence in the whisky trade. The answer lies in both the nature of the patent still and the character of the whisky produced in it. In principle the process of making grain whisky up to the stage of actual distillation is not dissimilar to that for malt whisky, with a mash of cereals being fermented in washbacks. But a patent still is an unlovely piece of industrial equipment, with none of the old-world cottage craft associations of the pot still. Distillation takes place in two tall columns, the analyser and the rectifier, which to the unscientific eye might equally well be used for fractionating – if that is the correct word – by-products of crude oil. As in the pot still, the spirit is vaporised and then condensed. Another difference between the two processes is that pot still distillation is a batch process, while in patent stills distillation is continuous.

The point at which the new spirit is condensed and collected is under the control of the stillman. It is perfectly possible to continue distilling until one is left with a neutral and flavourless alcohol. Indeed patent stills are used in many countries to distil neutral spirit, which after further distillation can then be turned into gin or vodka or any of half a dozen other ignoble drinks. The key issue is the point at which the spirit is collected from the patent still. This is where arguments start about what is or is not whisky, and where evasiveness tends to appear.

The definition of Scotch Whisky under British law is explicit on this issue. The whisky must have 'an aroma and flavour derived from the materials used' in its production and must be distilled at an alcoholic strength less than 94.8 per cent. All Scotch, whether it be single whiskies or blends, must conform to this definition.

Distillers in Scotland have no difficulty in meeting this legal requirement. However, in certain other countries whisky may by definition be a blend of whisky and neutral spirit. In the United States, for example, blended whisky may contain up to 80 per cent of neutral spirit. Distillers in these countries, jealous of the success of Scotch in penetrating their markets, have been quick to suggest that Scotch grain whisky is no more than a neutral spirit and that therefore blended Scotch is on a par with their own whiskies.

One cannot help feeling that the whisky trade in Scotland should have been more forthright in meeting this challenge. Not all that long ago, companies were reluctant to allow visitors to be shown round their patent still distilleries and even now one seldom finds grain whisky mentioned in their advertisements or publicity material. People should be told, unequivocally, that whisky made in patent stills in Scotland is genuine Scotch Whisky and that, like all Scotch, it is matured in casks made from oak for at least the minimum period prescribed by law.

Two patent still distilleries, Cameronbridge and Invergordon, do in fact bottle their whisky as single grain whisky,
and there is a demand for it. John Green, a film producer
who, by marrying Alison Bullen, deprived me of an irreplace-
able secretary, is only one of many whisky drinkers who
prefer single grain whisky to single malts or blends. Camer-
onbrig is the brand name for the grain whisky distilled at
Windygates in Fife. Unlike most grain whisky distilleries,
Cameronbridge is situated in a leafy glen and I can think of
no better place to visit and learn that distilling grain whisky is
not as mechanical and unromantic as one might suppose.
Invergordon distillery, on the Cromarty Firth, was built in
1961 by Frank Thomson, a colourful, extrovert character. For
him it was an act of faith, intended to bring employment to a
region where there was little alternative to agriculture and to
help halt the depopulation of the Highlands. Sceptics in the
whisky trade said Thomson was mad. Grain whisky had
always been made in the central belt of Scotland, in or around
the cities where blended Scotch Whisky was bottled and near
to ports from which it could easily be shipped to export
markets. To bring it down from the Highlands would be
uneconomic, they claimed.

At first it appeared as though Thomson's critics were right,
and for a decade or more Invergordon struggled through difficult times. The distillery was a single unit which had to rely
on other whisky companies buying its grain whisky to use in
their blends, and throughout the 1960s orders were slow to
come. The man who played a major part in resolving Invergordon's difficulties was Charles Craig, a bluff but sociable
Londoner, with a disarming habit of pretending to be more
innocent than he really is. Charles teamed up with Chris
Greig, a brilliantly clever distiller with probably a greater
expertise in the technical aspects of making whisky than

anyone in the trade. Together they turned Invergordon from a lone distillery into a whisky company, acquiring what financial analysts would no doubt describe as a portfolio of malt whisky distilleries on Speyside, Islay and Jura and finally the Edinburgh firm, Charles Mackinlay and Company, which had its own brand of blended Scotch Whisky, well established in both the home and export markets. Invergordon Distillers is now one of the major companies in the Scotch Whisky business.

If, on arriving at Edinburgh airport, one heads for the city centre not through Corstorphine, which is usually blocked with traffic, but using a new road built where there were once railway tracks, one's nose will suddenly be assailed by the heavy, though not unpleasant, smell of fermenting cereals. The smell might well be coming from one of several breweries in Edinburgh, but presently, as the road rises, one will see the buildings of the North British distillery, not a pretty sight at the best of times, and whenever I pass, there are always signs of building and reconstruction. One should not grumble at that, though, for it must mean that the distillery, and therefore a large number of whisky companies, are prospering.

'The NB', as it is affectionately called by everyone in the business, is a unique institution, a kind of distillers' cooperative. It was built in 1886 at a time when the Distillers Company Limited had a virtual monopoly of the grain whisky made in Scotland. So a number of smaller wine and spirit merchants and blending firms, the 'independents' as they later came to be called, pooled their resources and built their own patent still distillery.

To make sure that the control of the NB remained in the hands of these companies, its articles stipulated that only people working in the whisky business could be offered shares in it. Shareholders wishing to sell their shares had to sell them back to the company and, as an additional precaution, no shares were sold to anyone working for the D.C.L. or its satellite companies. In the more relaxed and amicable atmosphere of today's Scotch Whisky trade, it is easy to see a touch of paranoia behind these arrangements, but the NB has remained an outstandingly efficient and prosperous company, and an invitation to be a shareholder carried a prestige well beyond the value of the shares.

Every year at the conclusion of its Annual General Meeting, all NB shareholders and a number of guests are invited to a lunch, which for many years has been held at the George Hotel in the Edinburgh street of that name. The lunch is a special occasion, one of the major social events in the whisky scene, with a superb meal and carefully chosen wines. People say that a couple of weeks before the lunch the NB's board of directors sit down and eat through the menu, just to satisfy themselves that it meets the standard which members and guests have come to expect of the lunch.

It was against this background that one year I found myself sitting next to Peter Russell at the lunch. Peter is a whisky broker, a well known Edinburgh character, witty but outspoken. A vintage claret was one of the wines served at the lunch, and when Peter sipped it he turned to me sharply.

'This wine is corked,' he said. 'Let's call the waiter over.'

No doubt the claret was corked but, coward that I am, I would never have complained, preferring to leave it unfinished in my glass. To complain about anything at the NB lunch, I felt, would be little short of *lèse majesté*. The waiter came, and when he was told the wine was corked, took our glasses away, returning presently with another decanter of claret and fresh glasses. It was all done so discreetly that I am sure no one at any of the other tables in the room noticed.

It was the custom at NB lunches for malt whisky to be

placed on every table, for guests to drink with their coffee at the end of the meal. As at Scotch Whisky Association functions, this was served in decanters to avoid revealing the name of the whisky and thus giving offence to any of the members, many of whom were from companies which owned malt whisky distilleries. The whisky I poured myself was, I am almost certain, Glenmorangie, which is not too hard to identify. Suddenly I became aware that Peter was looking at his glass suspiciously.

'Heavens!' he exclaimed. 'What on earth is wrong with this whisky?'

'Now, Peter!' I protested.

To decide that the wine was corked was one thing, but if he was complaining about the whisky at the NB lunch, I would have nothing to do with it. And yet Peter knew his whiskies. Besides being in the broking business, his company blend and bottle Scotch. Its Isle of Skye is a very fine eight-year-old blend with an international reputation. When he saw my hesitation, Peter handed me his glass without comment. One sniff at it told me he was right. The whisky had the most extraordinary nose, with a heavy, perfumed sweetness overlying the familiar aroma of malt whisky.

'Have you added anything to the whisky?' I asked Peter.

'Only water from that decanter.'

I sniffed at the neck of the decanter by his left elbow and could not help laughing. For the first time in history, as far as I knew, decanters of gin as well as of malt whisky had been placed on all the tables at the lunch. It must have been the result of a mental aberration on the part of the hotel staff. No sane whisky distiller would ever dream of drinking gin with his coffee after a meal!

Apropos of grain whisky, Sandy Gordon once told a story which I will not repeat in detail, for what he described happened a good many years ago and there is nothing to be gained by blowing on the dying coals of an old animosity. The essence of it was that his company, which produces and markets Grant's blended whisky in addition to their two single malts, found itself in a dilemma. He had been told that if his company followed a certain course of action which the Distillers Company Limited believed would be against the best interests of the trade, it would supply William Grant's with no further supplies of grain whisky. Since the D.C.L. had a virtual monopoly of grain whisky production at the time, this would have meant when its stocks of grain whisky ran out, Grant's would no longer be able to produce its blend.

In the circumstances there was nothing the company could do except abandon its planned course of action, but the Grant family was determined that it should not again be in a position where it was vulnerable to that kind of pressure. So Sandy's brother Charles had a patent still distillery constructed at Girvan and it was completed in record time. Unlike most patent still distilleries which are located in industrial cities where conditions are cramped, it is on a greenfield site, and for those who wish to find out how grain whisky is made, it is well worth visiting.

Girvan is in Ayrshire, the county in which Robert Burns was born. Burns, an unwavering believer in independence, would surely have approved of the Grant family's resolute action. After all, did he not write that 'Freedom and whisky gang taegither'?

Richard Paterson, the master blender of Whyte and Mackay, the Glasgow whisky firm, handed me a nosing glass. It was one of five glasses on a table in front of us in his office and into each of which he had poured a sample of a different whisky with a little water added. I sniffed the glass and decided that the whisky did not seem in any way exceptional, rather bland on the nose, it seemed.

When I asked him what the whisky in the glass was, he replied, 'You could call it a mini-blend of well-aged whiskies, but Scapa is the predominating malt.'

He handed me three more of the glasses and I nosed them in turn. Two contained samples of Macallan single malt at different ages, nine and sixteen years as far as I recall, and both matured in sherry casks. The third was a sample of Longmorn, also matured in sherry wood. The difference between the whiskies was easy enough to detect though not easy to describe.

'Now nose the Scapa blend again,' Richard told me.

I did as he asked, and was amazed. This time there was, in the background as it seemed, an aroma that I had not noticed before, the salty tang of a whisky distilled by the sea, not nearly so pungent as in an Islay malt, but unmistakable all the same. Richard explained then that he had been demonstrating how the aroma one gets from a 20-year-old whisky can seem to change quite quickly once it is poured into a glass. I remembered then a conversation with another blender, Alan Reid of Robertson & Baxter, which I had had in his sample room in West Nile Street. Nosing a whisky, Alan had told me, could be an experience not unlike an optical illusion. If one looks long enough at a drawing of a cube, for example, it begins to change, until one has the impression that one is looking into an empty room. Similarly, people nosing a sample of whisky might at first only notice its smokiness, but then if they nose it again, they might believe they could detect other aromas, of heather honey, pear drops, black-currants.

A whisky blender may have to nose scores, hundreds even, of whisky samples during the course of his work. He works solely with his sense of smell, for otherwise he would not last the day. He is not looking for the aroma of blackcurrants or pear drops. To understand what he is looking for, we need to understand the fundamentals of blending. A blended whisky is composed of a number of single whiskies, malt as well as grain whiskies, blended together to the specification of a pre-determined formula. The number of single whiskies in a blend will vary, probably between fifteen and fifty, and, the ages at which they are used in the blend will also vary. No whisky can be used unless it has been matured in an oak cask for the minimum of three years, and if the age of a blended whisky is given on its label, it must be the age of the youngest single whisky in the blend; averaging is not allowed.

Just as the objective of a distiller is to produce a single whisky which remains consistent at all times, never varying in flavour or character, so the blender's ambition is to produce a blended Scotch whisky which also never varies. Some might think that this was an unnecessary refinement and that whisky drinkers would not notice small variations in the taste of a particular blend, especially as most people in a bar or pub do not order their whisky by brand name and simply ask for a Scotch. This is blatantly untrue, and I was once made aware of it in the bar of Edinburgh's Caledonian Hotel.

Frank was the barman there at the time. I do not believe I ever knew his surname, but he was courteous and dignified, one of the great fraternity of international barmen known to all those who prefer to take their drink in luxurious surround-ings and be impeccably served. I was alone, waiting for a friend, and I had ordered a Mackinlay's whisky. After a time Frank asked me, diffidently, whether Charles Mackinlay and Company, the owner of the brand, might have changed the composition of the blend. His reason for asking was that two of his regular customers, an Edinburgh man and his wife who never drank any whisky except Mackinlay's, had been in the bar earlier that evening. Frank had poured each of them a dram, and after tasting it they had asked him if he was sure he had given them Mackinlay's.

'I have the feeling,' Frank told me sadly, 'that they may have suspected that it was not Mackinlay's in the bottle from which I had served them.'

I understood the reason for Frank's hurt pride. It is not uncommon for unscrupulous barmen to fill empty bottles of a reputable brand of Scotch with less well-known and cheaper brands in order to increase their profits. Sometimes unscrupulous salesmen from whisky companies make it worth their while to do so. Frank, as I well knew, would never have been party to this kind of shoddy fraud and he did not like to be suspected of it.'

As it happened, a day or two later I ran into Donald Mackinlay, the fifth generation of his family to be the company's blender. When I repeated the story Frank had told me, he was amazed.

'I would never have believed that any ordinary drinker would have noticed the difference in our whisky!' he said.

'Then you have changed the blend?'

'Certainly not!'

He told me that a short time previously his company had decided to use a new type of filter in their bottling hall. Whisky must be filtered before it is bottled and the new filter now fitted in the company's bottling lines was known to be more effective than the type previously used. Before it had been installed, experiments had been tried, and Donald had believed that he could detect a change in the flavour of the blended whisky which had been passed through it. He had put his view to the other members of his blending team and to the other directors of the company, none of whom agreed with him. They could find no change whatever in the flavour of the blend. So the new filter had been accepted.

'It's extraordinary!' Donald exclaimed. 'The change in the flavour, if indeed there is one, is minute. I would never have believed that any member of the public would have noticed it.

'Perhaps you should recruit this man and his wife to your blending team,' I suggested facetiously.

A whisky blender and his assistants have to make sure that every cask of whisky must be ready for adding to the blend. The whisky must not be contaminated in any way. It sometimes happens, for example, that whisky is filled into a cask which, at some stage in its life, has been used not for sherry or bourbon whiskey, but for a liqueur. Over the years, any sweetness from the residue of the liqueur would penetrate the whisky and make it unusable. Similarly if the cask itself has deteriorated, the whisky might absorb the smell and flavour of the wood. Blenders must always be on the alert for any trace of woodiness in a single whisky.

Their responsibility does not end with checking the purity of the whisky. They must also decide if it has reached the required stage of maturity. For any of the number of reasons Sandy Curle and I had discussed at the Fiddichside Inn, whisky may take longer to mature and if it is not ready after, say, four years, the cask can be left in the warehouse for a further period of maturation.

Although Scotch Whisky is always blended to an established formula, and the quantity and age of the different single whiskies are taken into account when the company producing the blend orders its 'fillings' from the different distilleries, changes may, even so, have to be made before the blend is bottled. The orders for fillings are based on a forecast of what sales of the blend will be so many years ahead. Forecasting is notoriously difficult, governed as sales are by the economic climate, changes in Excise duties and the marketing achievements of competitive brands. So when the time comes to bottle the whisky, a company may find that it is short of a particular type of whisky or whiskies. In these cases the skill of the blender is crucial. If additional supplies of a single whisky are not available, he must know how he can compensate by using other whiskies or by changing the proportions of the other component whiskies and in this way adjust the blend to arrive at the same flavour.

Most whisky companies who produce and market blended Scotch, especially the larger ones, are likely to have more than one brand. They will probably have a standard blend and a premium or de luxe blend, and may well also market a secondary blend aimed at customers who wish to pay less for their Scotch. Some companies have special blends for sale only in certain countries overseas, where their experience or their market research have told them that people prefer a particular style of Scotch. In the 1960s many people in the whisky business appeared to believe that Americans preferred a 'light' Scotch – meaning by this not necessarily light in colour, but light in flavour – and that the blended Scotches that were selling particularly well in the States fell into this category.

No one to my knowledge has ever defined a 'light' Scotch, at least not with any degree of precision, so I can only give my impressions, or at least those of my senses of taste and smell. A light Scotch appears to have very little of the smokiness associated with more traditional blended Scotches, suggesting that little if any peat has been used in the production of its component single whiskies. One would also think that the malt whiskies chosen to make up the blend would be those with a more delicate and less obtrusive character, excluding the Islay malts and the more robust of the Highland malts as well as any malts matured in sherry wood. There might also be a suspicion that light blends contain a higher proportion of grain whisky, though those who produce light blends would probably be reluctant to admit this.

Any discussion of the balance between malt and grain whiskies in a blend must also be approached with tact and delicacy, for it is a no-man's land of conflicting perceptions and prejudices. Most people accept that in principle it is the malt whiskies that give a blend most of its flavour. On the basis of this premise, it is understandable that they would assume that the greater the proportion of malt whisky in a blend, the better it will be. Such an assumption would not necessarily be correct. A blend made up of say 80 per cent of single malt whiskies and 20 per cent of grain whiskies might well not be any better than a blend in which these proportions are reversed. Indeed, such a blend might well be less acceptable to most whisky drinkers.

This immediately begs the question of what makes a good blended Scotch and how the blender goes about creating one. James Bruxner, the Chairman of Justerini and Brooks, draws an analogy between a blended Scotch and a concert orchestra playing a symphony. The instruments in the orchestra will perform differently, some playing *forte*, some so *pianissimo* that they can scarcely be heard, but the result will be a perfect balance.

I prefer to compare a blender to a hostess arranging a dinner party. She would decide first who were to be the principal guests, the attractions of the evening. The other guests must be carefully chosen. They would not be noisy extroverts who would interrupt the flow of conversation, but modest, undemanding people who would play a supporting role, asking the questions and making the comments that would bring the best out of the lions. Only in this way could she ensure an enjoyable and memorable evening.

A good blend then should be a balance between the more strongly flavoured single malt whiskies, which will give it its character and others of a more equable temperament, Lowland malts and grains, which will make their contribution by enhancing and bringing the best out of the principals. Most blenders would agree that no single whisky should dominate a blend.

In Bessie Campbell's day her company, besides bottling Laphroaig as a single malt, marketed a blend named Islay Mist. Unusually for blended whiskies, the label on the bottle stated that it was a blend of three single malts and grain whisky. The malts were all outstanding in their categories. As far as I recall they were The Glenlivet, Glenfarclas and, of course, Laphroaig. Yet the blend was so dominated by the pungent flavour of Laphroaig that it was unlikely to appeal to any whisky drinkers other than *aficionados* of Islay whisky.

Similarly it used to be said a few years ago that one could always detect the flavour of Lagavulin in White Horse blended Scotch. White Horse, named incidentally after a howf or inn in Edinburgh frequented by Robert Burns, had first been put on the market by Peter Mackie who at the time owned Lagavulin distillery, so this was not altogether surprising. But the general feeling in the whisky trade was that there was too much Lagavulin in the blend. This does not appear to be true of White Horse today, so perhaps the blend has been adjusted.

Whisky blenders do not rank all whiskies equally. Many of them will list the single malt whiskies in order of merit. There might be grades of Highland malt whiskies, from one down to five, with separate categories for Lowland malts and Islay malts. Whisky brokers would have similar lists, since the price that a mature single whisky would command in the broking market would depend on its ranking. The lists of different blenders are unlikely to be the same, since the merits of a single whisky, for blending as well as drinking, is a matter of personal judgment.

A distiller whom I know well was at one time angry to see that in one list his distillery's whisky was ranked as a fourth category Highland malt.

'Everyone in the trade agrees that it is at least a third category malt,' he complained to me. 'In fact, more than one blender places it in category two.'

In spite of this, a glance at different lists will show that there is a high degree of consensus. With the proliferation of bottled single malts on the market and the sometimes extravagant compliments that are paid to them by wine writers, these distinctions are in danger of being forgotten. Anyone who is a newcomer to the pleasures of malt whisky is likely to be influenced by a remark like, 'This is a splendid and largely unknown single malt which I have discovered, made in a tiny distillery on the southern slopes of Ben Hype.'

The choice of a hostess when planning her dinner party is limited by the number of her friends. For a whisky blender, on the other hand, the number of permutations open to him are virtually limitless. Not only can he choose from more than a hundred different single whiskies, but he can use them at different stages of maturation. Then he has a choice between whiskies matured in sherry casks and those that have been kept in former bourbon casks, or a combination of the two. The type of warehouse in which the whisky has matured gives another, though much less pronounced, variation in flavour.

Using all the permutations at its disposal a whisky

company could, if it wished, produce literally thousands of blends, all differing in flavour and character. So producing a blend especially for one particular market presents no problem. In the last few years 'own label' blended whiskies have also developed into a substantial and profitable business for those companies who specialise in them.

Originally these blends were produced mainly for exclusive institutions and clubs. Some years ago in the bottling halls of James Buchanan and Sons just outside Glasgow I remember seeing the House of Commons blend, which it produced for the refreshment department of the House, going along the bottling line. Not long afterwards I was fortunate enough to be given a bottle by Ian Campbell, the Member of Parliament for Dumbarton, who was one of a number of Scottish MPs who recognised the importance of Scotch to the economy of Scotland and worked hard to defend the interests of the industry at Westminster. The bottle has an attractive label with a representation of a portcullis, symbol of the House of Commons, in green against a white background. The blend was completely different from Buchanan's Black and White. No doubt it still is, because the company continues to supply the House of Commons with whisky. British Rail also used to have its own blend, and so did Harrods. Today some of the larger supermarkets sell their own brands of Scotch, and these will usually be blended specially for them by a whisky company.

A number of whisky companies also supply 'own label' Scotch to a wide range of private clubs and restaurants, and generally they will accept any order, provided it is large enough to make it economic. A significant number of private label blends are even bottled for private individuals. In the normal way the company does not produce a blend specially for the customer, but will send him samples of say three or four blends which they have on offer. The customer chooses one and decides on the shape of bottle and the design of label he would like. The whisky is then blended, bottled and despatched to the customer, leaving him only the tiresome formality of paying, not only for its cost but whatever Excise Duty prevails in his country, before he can produce it to impress his friends.

The blender's is a highly skilled craft. Just to have a well developed sense of smell is not enough. Trevor Cowan, who works with Donald Mackinlay as a blender for Mackinlays, has explained better than anyone I know the most exacting part of a blender's virtuosity. He or she – the number of women blenders is growing – must be able to lock into his memory, like sensory filing cards, the 'nose' he would expect from a single whisky, malt or grain. Every whisky blender would not necessarily be able to identify any sample of a single, unblended whisky you put before him and, of course, if you were to include all the hundreds of different blends, the task would be impossible. Even so, the ability to identify different whiskies is extraordinary and it is not confined to blenders.

I was once present at a reception organised by the Scotch Whisky Association for a party of visitors from the Continent in Edinburgh's Caledonian Hotel, which at the time was owned by British Railways. As always at Association functions, instructions had been given to the hotel that the Scotch should be served in decanters to avoid embarrassment. It had also been stipulated that any brands of Scotch might be served, provided that they belonged to members of the Association. This excluded, as it was meant to do, the British Railways brand, Royal Scot, which was a perfectly acceptable whisky, but the railways were not members of the Association.

Bill Burnett, the Production Director of the Distillers

Company, was one of the early arrivals at the reception. He took no more than one sip of the glass of Scotch that was handed to him and then said, loudly, for he was a little deaf, 'Why are we being given Royal Scot?' The head waiter was called. He looked embarrassed but made no attempt to deny that the whisky was Royal Scot. No doubt it had been a genuine mistake on the part of the hotel's staff, or the instructions had not reached them. The offending decanters of whisky were removed to be replaced by others containing a brand owned by a member of the Association. I found it remarkable that Bill Burnett should have been able at once to recognise a Scotch which was not one of his company's brands and which he would seldom drink.

The sample room of a whisky company is a fascinating place. Ranged along its walls are glass-fronted cupboards holding hundreds of bottles containing samples of different whiskies, malts, grains and blends. The bottles are plain, even less attractive than medicine bottles, and each will carry a label on which will be written the make of whisky, the date when it was distilled and its cask number. A working table in the centre of the room is fitted with a tap and a sink and on it there will be rows of sample glasses, tulip shaped to allow a concentration of the aroma from the whisky at the neck.

The blender will pour a little of the whisky he wishes to examine into a glass, add an equal quantity of water to release the aroma and then sniff at the neck of the glass. One sniff is usually enough to tell him what he wants to know, but a second and more prolonged sniff may be needed, or he may pass it to a colleague in the blending team for his opinion. In some sample rooms one may see a set of sample glasses made from blue glass. These are used, though very rarely, in cases where the blender does not want the colour of the whisky to affect his judgment.

Blenders often wear white coats while they are working, and this reinforces the disappointingly clinical appearance of the sample room. One might be watching scientists at work in a laboratory, dispassionately examining the liquid by-products of coal or petroleum. Then the blender will hand you samples to nose, and just as the glasses will release the aroma of Cardhu or Bruichladdich or Ben Nevis, so will the aroma release your imagination and you can smell the fragrances of the glens and the moors.

Sample rooms must in any case be clinical or at least clinically clean. Any conflicting scents or smells make it impossible to nose a whisky accurately. You may have noticed that if you have shaken hands with a girl wearing perfume, her perfume will have passed from her hands on to yours and then, if you raise a glass of Scotch to your lips, the scent of the perfume will clash with the flavour of the whisky. For this reason blenders generally do not like people who are wearing any form of scent to come into the sample room. They know that the scent will linger long after the visitor has left.

The skill of the blender in detecting and interpreting the subtle differences in whiskies gives his work a special fascination. The practicalities of actually blending the single whiskies together to make a blended Scotch, on the other hand, are prosaic if not banal. Blending and bottling halls are unappealing places and the scale of their operations do not encourage any romantic impressions. Traditionally the casks of all the single whiskies are rolled into the blending hall and lined up beside the blending trough. The bungs are then removed and the casks tipped one by one to discharge the whisky into the trough, along which it will pass to the blending vats.

Each cask will have stencilled on one end the name of the distillery from which the whisky has come, together with the year in which it was distilled. By walking along the rows of casks awaiting disgorging in the blending hall one can get a fair idea of which single whiskies go to make up the blend. Taking a note pad and jotting down the names as you pass would not be encouraged, though.

Even this insight into the composition of a blend is not now always possible. Some whisky companies no longer bring whisky down from the distilleries where it has been maturing in casks, but have it filled at the distilleries into tankers, which transplant it in bulk to the blending halls. Grain whisky and malt whisky are brought in separately and discharged into the blending vats. The casks are left at the distillery to be refilled with new whisky.

In the blending vats the whisky is thoroughly roused or stirred. It may then be filled into casks once more and left in a warehouse for a further period, allowing the single whiskies in the blend time to settle down, or 'marry', as they say. The blend is then filtered, bottled and packed in cases in modern automatic bottling lines. Bottling halls are noisy places, with the constant chink of bottle against bottle and the only sense of wonder one can have is at the sophistication of the machinery. In the most modern plant which I have seen, Ballantine's at Kilmalid in Dumbartonshire, more than 265 bottles can be filled, labelled and cased in one minute. Only mechanisation of this order had enabled the whisky industry to cope with the growing demand for Scotch.

Before blended whisky is bottled, colour in the form of caramelised sugar may be added to it. This is another controversial issue, though some would think scarcely a major one. The objective of adding colour is simply to achieve consistency. With the best will in the world it is impossible simply by blending to produce a whisky which will always have precisely the same shade, for the colour of the single whiskies in the blend will vary according to their length of maturation and the type of cask used. Whisky companies believe that customers would be disconcerted if the colour of a brand of Scotch were to change and would assume that the blend itself had been changed. Only minute quantities of colour may be added, a pint or two in thousands of gallons of whisky. Most people in the trade do not believe that this can make any difference to the flavour, but there are some who will swear that it does and that the whisky is sweeter. If whisky drinkers as a whole had a better understanding of both distilling and blending, colour would not be needed.

Before bottling, whisky is 'reduced' in strength by adding water to it. The strength of whisky – and of other spirits – is a subject which mystifies most people, and with good reason. Proof strength was the standard measurement in Britain until 1980, but this caused more confusion than enlightenment, with people in the trade talking of 'over proof' and 'under proof' and America having its own system of proof which was different, although marginally more logical than ours.

Let us start at the beginning, which means going back in time. The way of measuring the strength of spirits dates back at least two centuries. The earliest method involved mixing a little of the spirit with gunpowder and then setting fire to the mixture. If it ignited with a suitable *éclat*, this was proof that it was of the required strength. If, on the other hand, it spluttered and fizzled out tamely, the spirit would be rejected. History does not record what happened if a man's eyebrows were blown off.

All one can say in favour of the system is that it was a good deal less ludicrous than the method of 'conning' the strength of ale. In this, the ale conner was required first to put on a pair of leather breeches. He would then pour the ale to be tested over a wooden bench and sit in it. His degree of difficulty in rising from the bench was a gauge of the ale's strength.

Several ways of measuring proof were devised to follow gunpowder. A set of distillers' beads of different sizes would be put into the spirit and, according to whether they floated or sank, would indicate its specific gravity, from which its strength could be calculated using a set of tables. The hydrometer, invented in the 1780s, fulfilled the same function.

Bureaucrats are not permitted to have a sense of fun, nor does romance appeal to them, so after the United Kingdom joined the European Community our system of proof vanished and was replaced by the OIML system, which means strength as a percentage of alcohol by volume at a temperature of 20° Centigrade. Measured by this method, malt whisky is usually taken off the still at around 70 per cent volume. Grain whisky is distilled to a much higher strength, which may be as high as 94.8 per cent. Both types of whisky will normally be reduced to about 64 per cent volume before being filled into casks for maturation by the addition of water, and may lose strength while they are maturing. They will be further reduced before blending and the normal strength is 40 per cent volume for the home market but 43 per cent for some export markets.

Anyone who has, without thinking, added tap water to his Scotch in the south of England, where the water is full of calcium and is heavily chlorinated, will know how this can ruin the flavour of the whisky. Water used to reduce whisky in the bottling halls must be soft and free of impurities. Several of the industry's bottling halls are in or around Glasgow, where the water is mainly drawn from Loch Katrine, said to be one of the finest waters to be found anywhere in Scotland. Companies bottling their whisky in less favoured locations may use demineralised water, or at least have it available to use if the local water supply should at any time fail to reach the standards required.

So, once more, water plays a vital role as it has done at every stage in the making of Scotch. Whisky is made in many parts of the world, but in no way does it resemble Scotch Whisky. In some countries laborious efforts have been made to distill a whisky that might in flavour and character be mistaken for Scotch. Distilleries have been constructed that are exact replicas of those on Speyside, processes have been copied in precise detail, peat has even been imported from Scotland to be used in malting, in the hope that this will provide the answer, but whiskies made in these lands remain different, no doubt perfectly drinkable and wholesome, but different.

What people often overlook is that it is not only the water and the barley and the peat that gives Scotch its unique flavour. Scotland is a northern country. Aberdeen is nearer to Stavanger in Norway than to London, and Shetland is on the same latitude as Alaska. Yet, because of the Gulf Stream which washes its west coast, palm trees and tropical flowers flourish not far north of Glasgow. The climate of Scotland, the air, the humidity, a reasonably stable temperature without extremes of hot or cold, are as important to the making of whisky as the water. These gifts of nature nobody can imitate.

6

The French Connection

In one way or another Scotland owes much to France. That the French now drink more Scotch than any other foreigners except the Americans may be one reason for gratitude, but it is itself a consequence of two other reasons of more ancient pedigree. The Auld Alliance between the Scots and the French is, in the minds of many people, vaguely associated with Mary Queen of Scots and her marriage to the Dauphin of France. In fact the alliance was formed much earlier than that, in 1295, to give the Scots protection against Edward I of England, who had already ravaged Wales and subjugated Ireland and had megalomaniac designs on Scotland.

As a result of the Auld Alliance, the Scots and the French were brought closer together and the manners of the Scottish court and nobility were much influenced by French culture and sophistication. A young Scot wishing to complete his education by travelling would go not to England but to France. It was in any case easier and safer to take ship for France from the east of Scotland than to risk the long journey by coach or on horseback to London. In France, too, Scots were treated as equals and not, as they were by the English, with scorn or contempt.

France also benefitted from the alliance, as the Scots developed a taste for French wines and brandies. In the eighteenth century more claret and burgundy were being drunk in Scotland than in England, and when illicit distilling was at its peak in the Highlands, large quantities of French brandy were being smuggled into the country. There is a well authenticated story of Excise Officers, accompanied by soldiers, arriving in the Solway Firth and finding a 'landing' of smuggled brandy taking place. Two luggers were involved, both lying off shore and both equipped with cannon. The leaders of the smugglers threatened the Excise Officers that, if they interfered, the ships would fire on them. If, on the other hand, they would agree to withdraw and allow the landing to be completed uninterrupted, casks of brandy would be left on the beach. The officers withdrew, and when they returned some time later they found thirty-six small casks waiting for them.

Within ten years of the 1823 Excise Act being passed grain whisky was being distilled in Scotland on a huge scale. This had been made possible by the invention by Robert Stein of the patent still in 1827 and its subsequent improvement by Aeneas Coffey three years later. Not long afterwards someone had the idea of mixing pot still and patent still whiskies and launched the era of blended Scotch Whisky.

No one knows with certainty who first blended whisky. Andrew Usher has generally been given the credit. Usher, an Edinburgh man, was an agent for Smith's Glenlivet and he began marketing vatted malt whisky, that is a mixture of either different distillations of the same single malt or different single malts. He is known to have marketed the first vatted malt, Usher's Old Vatted Glenlivet, in 1853. Brodie Hepburn, a Glasgow whisky broker, presented me with a half bottle of Usher's that had been given to him by his father, also a well-known whisky man, and which must have been bottled very early in this century. I still have the bottle, though Donald Mackinlay and I could not resist the tempt-ation of drawing the cork and pouring a tiny quantity of the whisky for us to examine. It was still excellent, even though it had lost a little colour.

The claim that Usher started blending is not unchallenged. Alexander Cameron of John Dewar and Sons, if he was not actually the first to blend malt and grain whiskies together, perfected the art of blending as it is known today. Cameron was a tireless experimenter, who learned that all single whiskies are not compatible and perfected a combination of forty of them, grain as well as malt, which became Dewar's White Label blend. Whatever the truth may be, there can be no denying that the development of the patent still and the introduction of blending, unpopular though they were among many distillers at the time, marked the beginning of the modern Scotch Whisky industry.

France influenced its early growth in two ways. It was the wine merchants in Scotland, who had built their business on the import of French wines and brandies and understood the retail and wholesale trade, who first saw the possibilities of selling Scotch Whisky outside the country. Until that time, whisky had mainly been sold in casks to public houses and dram shops in Scotland, where it was dispensed by the glass. Large quantities of both pot still and patent still whisky were being shipped to England, but it was almost all being rectified and made into gin.

Scotch was scarcely known in England, where gin and porter were the tipples of working people, while the leisured classes preferred brandy. Brandy and soda was the drink a hostess would offer guests towards the end of an evening, during which they would have had sherry or madeira as an aperitif and wine with their dinner, and the men would drink port after the ladies had withdrawn from the dinner table. Brandy and soda was also what men would drink as they played cards at their London clubs.

Then a series of minor disasters hit the French wine trade. A form of mildew began to affect the vineyards, bringing a succession of poor crops. To counter this the French imported vine stocks from America, in the expectation that this good new 'blood' would restore the health of their vines. Instead they found they had imported a major disaster, an aphid related to greenfly, called phylloxera. In 1879 this immigrant began to ravage the vineyards of France, destroying more than half her wine. Wine became scarce as well as expensive and so, of course, did French brandy.

Whisky blenders in Scotland were quick to take advantage of the situation and began promoting the merits of Scotch. The suggestion, sometimes made, that this misfortune of the French was solely responsible for the switch in the tastes of the English and the beginning of the world popularity of Scotch is an over-simplification. By 1879 there was already a substantial trade in blended whisky with England, and several Scottish wine merchants had agents in Liverpool, Newcastle and Hull. The Glasgow firm of William Teacher and Sons had representation in London by 1876, while the Kilmarnock firm of John Walker opened a London branch in 1880. Blended Scotch was also being exported to Australia, New Zealand, India and South Africa; in fact to almost every country where expatriate Scots had settled and were thirsty for their native drink.

The royal family of England may also have helped indirectly to endorse the respectability of Scotch as a drink. Prince Albert had taken a liking to Balmoral, which he compared with the central European duchy whence he came and, in fact, they were about the same size. Albert took to wearing the kilt and insisting that, while in Scotland, his children should do the same. An old photograph shows a family group, the boys looking as uncomfortable in Highland dress as they might have done in grass skirts.

Whether it was admiration of Scotland or of her man-servant John Brown that attracted Queen Victoria to Scotland is not clear, but the middle class *nouveaux riches* followed her there, buying houses and sporting estates and discovering that whisky was really quite a palatable drink.

Even before then George IV, on a visit to Edinburgh in 1822 – he was the first reigning sovereign courageous enough to face the Scots at home for a hundred and fifty years – expressed a wish to drink whisky. He insisted on having malt whisky from the Highlands, for that was before the advent of blending, and grain whisky made in the Lowlands had a poor reputation. In her *Memoirs of a Highland Lady*, Elizabeth Grant of Rothiemurchus tells how she reluctantly sent some of her stocks of Glenlivet whisky, together with thirty brace of ptarmigan, to Holyrood Palace for the king. The whisky, she said, had the real 'contraband gout', but the reference to the fact that she kept it in uncorked bottles is puzzling. Anyway her father was later given a judgeship in India as a reward for her gesture.

In support of blended Scotch Whisky it is sometimes claimed that malt whisky is too heavy to appeal to drinkers living in warmer climes or working in sedentary occupations. Pot still malt whisky, some people declare, is a drink for the grouse moors and the salmon rivers and for those who work out of doors in Scotland's rugged climate. The early blenders are given the credit for realising this and for intentionally producing a blend of malts and grains which, being lighter in character, would have more appeal in England as well as in overseas markets.

This is another of the myths that have grown up, or been invented, about Scotch Whisky. Although subsequent events have shown that the worldwide success has been based on blended whisky, one can scarcely believe that those who first blended Scotch had the prescience with which some are ready to credit them. In the 1870s malt whisky was flourishing, relatively at least, and was being exported to a number of countries overseas, particularly Australia and South Africa, where there was a preference for strongly flavoured and even fiery malt whiskies. Patent still grain whisky, on the other hand, was going through a difficult time. Over-production had created problems which were exacerbated by government policy. English distillers of 'plain British spirits' used in the manufacture of gin had demanded protection against imports of spirits from Scotland. They had been given this by regulations of one type or another and by frequent changes in the system of levying Excise Duties, which had the effect of discriminating against Scottish patent still distillers.

Faced with these difficulties, one patent still distillery, the Caledonian in Edinburgh, even installed two large pot stills just to produce an Irish-style whisky that would appeal to the large numbers of Irish immigrants in Scotland. Six of the largest patent still distilleries united under the name of the

Distillers Company Limited in 1877. Public confidence in patent still whisky was not high, and only a tiny proportion of the shares put on the market by the new company were subscribed.

Knowing these circumstances, it is difficult not to believe that blending pot still and patent still whiskies was started primarily as a matter of commercial expediency, to produce a drink which would be used to absorb the surplus capacity of patent stills yet still have a flavour resembling that of malt whisky. In order to achieve this resemblance, these early blends were composed mainly of the more strongly flavoured island whiskies and those distilled near the Spey, the Glen-livets as they were called, together with grain whisky which might make up as much as ninety-five per cent of the blend.

As one might expect, the development of blended Scotch Whisky and its gradual acceptance over the following two decades were strongly resented by pot still distillers, who saw sales of their unblended malt whiskies decline. Some of them were far-sighted enough to realise that a growing demand for blends would in the long term be to their advantage, but even so they pressed the government to lay down regulations requiring a minimum malt whisky content in all blends.

Their position was slowly being weakened as some of the larger blenders, such as James Buchanan and John Haig and Company, bought pot still distilleries to safeguard their supplies of malt whisky. Even a London wine merchant, W. & A. Gilbey, had bought a malt whisky distillery at Rothes. The price of malt whisky was forced down, causing some distillers to sell out and others to go into liquidation.

The dispute and the lobbying continued with increasing bitterness and flared up in 1905 when the Borough of Islington in London decided to prosecute two wine and spirit firms for selling whisky which was not of 'the nature, substance and quality demanded'. The magistrates, in what came to be known as the 'What is Whisky?' case, ruled in favour of the Borough Council, causing panic among the patent still distillers and whisky blenders. The battle-lines were now drawn.

The chairman of the Distillers Company Limited, William Ross, proposed a compromise, and blenders were prepared to negotiate a minimum content of pot still whisky in all blends, but agreement could not be reached. The pot still distillers wanted a minimum of forty per cent and the blenders would probably have settled for a minimum of thirty per cent, but the pot still distillers were also insisting that all whisky should be matured for a minimum of two years. This would have added greatly to the cost of patent still grain whisky, most of which was not matured at all.

Finally, in 1908, the government was persuaded by the Distillers Company to appoint a Royal Commission to examine the whole subject of whisky and other potable spirits. The Commission was composed of six scientific and medical experts, all Sassenachs who knew almost nothing about whisky, with Lord James of Hereford as chairman. They spent a year listening to the elaborate arguments put forward by pot still distillers on the one hand and patent still distillers on the other. In its report, the Commission carefully avoided reaching any decision on either what minimum proportion of malt whisky there should be in a blend or on any period of compulsory maturation for whisky. Instead it contented itself with giving a broad and largely anodyne definition of whisky and stated that no further legislation was needed. In effect the report represented a complete victory for the patent still distillers and the blenders.

The Commission's report was attacked at the time and later by many prominent Scots. In retrospect one can see now that, although it stirred passion and alarm, it was no more than a hiccough in the development of blended Scotch Whisky. The identity of the first person to blend malt and grain whiskies may not be known, but it was the wine merchants of the day, now names known throughout the world – Walker, Buchanan, Dewar and Gloag – who promoted it and with their enterprise and flair began the train of events which led to blended Scotch Whisky becoming the most popular spirit drink in the world.

One evening twelve men sat down to dine in the ornate restaurant of one of London's finest hotels. All were wearing evening dress, including the slim tall red-haired Scot, who looked as though he might have been more at home in a kilt. The wine waiter came to the table and asked them what they would care to drink before their dinner.

'Buchanan's Blend whisky, of course!' the man at the head of the table replied.

The wine waiter, embarrassed, told him that the hotel had no Buchanan's whisky.

'What? No Buchanan's?' the party exclaimed aghast and very loudly. The timing and intonation of their chorus were impeccable, for with one exception they were all actors, hired for the occasion. Having made it clear to all the other diners in the room that they could not possibly dine at any establishment which did not carry Buchanan's whisky, they rose and left the room indignantly, heading for another hotel or restaurant where they could put on an encore of their performance.

The performance was only one of many devices – certainly not the most subtle but a relatively inexpensive one – used by the red-haired Scot to promote his whisky. James Buchanan was born in Canada of immigrant Scottish parents, who soon after his birth returned to Scotland. After working as a shipping clerk and then for a grain merchant, he went to London at the age of thirty as a representative of the whisky merchant and blender, Charles Mackinlay and Sons of Leith. It has been said that he was not very successful, but even so after five years he was satisfied that he had acquired the knowledge and experience needed to form his own company. With borrowed capital and a guarantee from the Glasgow firm of W.P. Lowrie that it would provide the whisky he needed, James Buchanan and Company was founded in London.

In later years Buchanan wrote that he was astonished at the 'supreme self-confidence' that had allowed him to embark on such an enterprise. One cannot dispute that judgment, but in addition to self-confidence, Buchanan possessed exactly those attributes needed to achieve his remarkable success: patience, persistence, vanity and sheer cheek. He used them to sell his whisky, driving around London in a brightly painted buggy and cultivating any connection which might help him in his business.

Two contacts he was able to make were of tremendous value to him. One secured him the contract to supply his whisky to most of the leading music halls in London, which were owned by one company. The other helped him to become a supplier of whisky to the House of Commons. That he was able to penetrate those two such contrasting social milieux is an indication of how swiftly blended Scotch Whisky was finding acceptance. James Buchanan and Company continued to supply Westminster with whisky, and as far as I know they still do, but under another label.

Buchanan late in his life told stories of how he had managed to 'land' these and other prized contracts, but he told them in such a way that gives the impression he was mainly concerned to emphasise his own shrewdness and business acumen. As a result, they often do not reflect well on his sincerity. One such story tells how, by befriending the two daughters of a lonely widower who owned a number of licensed houses in London, he managed to win an order for 5,000 gallons of his whisky, which he later was able to turn into an exclusive contract.

His stories probably do him an injustice, for he would scarcely have been as well liked as he evidently was, if he had been as cynically self-seeking as the stories make him appear. The truth may be that Buchanan was proud of his salesmanship. There is no reason why he should not have been, for he was one of the leaders among a new species, marketing men who used their ingenuity to find ways of promoting what they wished to sell. He was the first to use many ploys which have since become routine: persuading newspapers to give Buchanan's Blend 'puffs' in their editorial columns by printing stories of celebrities who would drink no other whisky, and getting medical men to lend their names to endorsements of its health-giving and restorative properties. Brand publicity was a new field in the whisky trade, for until the advent of blending there were no brand names to publicise. Buchanan used all his energy to get 'exposure' for his brand, later renamed Black and White, in the best hotels, restaurants and clubs and at social occasions.

Buchanan's new type of salemanship was very successful, and in a relatively short time he had built up his company to a point when it had opulent offices in Holborn, on the site of the historic Black Swan distillery. Its fleet of vans, drawn by superb black horses and driven by coachmen in livery, soon became a spectacle in the city. Like many self-made men, he used horse-racing as an entrée to the social circles of the aristocracy and became a successful owner, with two Derby winners among his horses, bred at Lavington Park in Sussex.

He was made a baronet in 1920 and two years later offered a peerage by Lloyd George. This was the subject of another story, which might be apocryphal but is typical of the stories which Buchanan told against himself. The peerage, it was said, was to be awarded to him in return for a substantial donation to Lloyd George's party fund. He was not averse to paying in advance but, mistrustful of politicians, signed his cheque 'Woolavington', the title he had chosen for himself, thus ensuring that it could not be cashed until the peerage had been announced in the official gazette.

In 1891 a firm of wine merchants in Perth, founded more than forty years previously by the son of a crofter from the village of Aberfeldy, received a letter which read:

Cluny Castle, September 21 1891

Messers John Dewar & Sons
    Merchants
      Perth

Gentlemen:

Can you get a small keg, say nine or ten gallons, of the best Scotch Whisky you can find, and ship it addressed as follows;

To the President,
    The Honourable Benjamin Harrison,
      Executive Mansion,
        Washington D.C.,
          U.S.A.

Send bill to me.

Yours Very Truly

Andrew Carnegie

Carnegie was a Scot who had emigrated to the United States and, having made a fortune in steel and friends of Presidents, returned to Scotland to lead the life of, if not a laird, then at least a Scottish gentleman. His request to the Perth firm of wine and spirit merchants seems odd for two reasons. One was that firms sending whisky abroad had found that in general it did not appear to travel well when shipped by sea in cask. The second reason for surprise is that Dewar's were one of the first, if not actually *the* first, whisky firm to blend Scotch and sell it in bottle. It is possible, one supposes, that Andrew Carnegie in the remote vastness of his castle might not have known this.

John Dewar, who started the modest shop in Perth, was the son of a crofter who farmed just outside Aberfeldy. He died in 1880 and the firm was taken over by his two sons, John Alexander and Thomas Robert. They decided that London offered the best potential market for blended Scotch Whisky and in 1887 Tom Dewar went south to conquer it. Inevitably he and James Buchanan, who had already launched himself on the same enterprise, became fierce rivals.

The two men were very different both in physique and in their style of salemanship. Buchanan was slim and handsome and, perhaps because he was a self-made man, he attached more importance to the elegance of dress and manners associated with the society of which he aspired to become a member. In photographs Tom Dewar has the look of a solid, forthright man with the build of a Rugby hooker. One might observe that there is nothing wrong with that. John Macphail, who as chairman of the Scotch Whisky Association in the 1980s, did as much as anyone ever has to protect and promote the interests of the Scotch Whisky industry, hooked for Scotland. Dewar's salesmanship was not as subtle as Buchanan's, based on a more direct approach and a refusal to be rebuffed, but he must have had considerable charm, for he received few rebuffs.

He had his greatest success abroad, in North America and the British Empire, where many Scots had settled or were working. It might even have been Andrew Carniege's letter which inspired him to explore export markets for his whisky, since it was in the year after receiving it that he embarked on a sales trip. It was to last two years and take him round the world, visiting more than twenty countries in which he established more than thirty agencies for Dewar's whisky. By the time he returned to London, orders were pouring into Perth from all over the world.

The voyage is well documented, for Dewar described it in his book, *A Ramble Round the Globe*. It carried more than two hundred illustrations by Royal Academicians and other established artists as well as some of his own sketches. He was an accomplished after-dinner speaker and this gift, together with his literary aspirations, found expression in aphorisms, some of which even found their way into contemporary anthologies. They reflect an innate but often witty cynicism, as for example 'The biggest lies are told on tombstones.' Another equally well known, 'Do right and fear no man; don't write and fear no woman', was perhaps what one might have expected from a bachelor.

Dewar became immensely popular in London, mainly because of his interest in sport. Like Buchanan he was a successful racehorse owner, but he also owned greyhounds, was a patron of amateur football and was one of the first men to buy a motor car in Britain. It was a huge Benz, and Dewar used to say that its highest running cost was hiring teams of horses to tow it back home when it broke down. He was a close friend of Thomas Lipton, the tea magnate, who had a passion for sailing and whose yacht *Shamrock* was a challenger for the America's Cup.

A rather nice story about the two of them is of a business trip Dewar made to Africa. During it he jokingly cabled to Lipton that he would be able to buy three wives for six pounds of Lipton's tea and suggesting that Lipton, also a bachelor, should go out there. Lipton telegraphed back, 'I am sending samples of tea. Please send me samples of wives.'

Dewar's salesmanship made the firm's White Label blend the most widely drunk Scotch at the turn of the century. The company could scarcely expand fast enough to keep pace with demand. It built a malt whisky distillery at Aberfeldy, still a model of its kind, and began buying others. In Dewar House, the firm's London offices in the Haymarket, it received its agents and distributors from all over the world. There in the handsome Edwardian building, they could see something of Scotland's cultural heritage, famous paintings including Landseer's *The Macnab* and *Monarch of the Glen* and the tavern table at which Robert Burns wrote many of his poems. Sadly, Dewar House was not long ago surrendered.

Like Buchanan and his brother John, Tom Dewar was first knighted and then given a peerage. They and others in the whisky business who were given titles came to be known, with perhaps as much envy as scorn, as the Whisky Barons. In those days honours were more often given in recognition of philanthropy than for public services, but in a later age Dewar would certainly have been entitled to his for his services to industry. He did more than any other single individual in his day certainly and perhaps ever, to make the name and the merits of Scotch Whisky internationally known.

The companies of Buchanan and Dewar were two of what came to be known as 'The Big Three' in the whisky trade. The third, John Walker and Sons, founded earlier than the other two in the Royal Burgh of Kilmarnock, was the first to open an office in London, though not with any immediate success and it was slow in doing any business. Ultimately, however, its two brands of blended Scotch Whisky, Johnnie Walker Red and Black Labels, outstripped all its competitors to become in world terms the largest selling Scotches in their categories. Alec Walker, grandson of the founder, was knighted for his services to the country during the First World War, when he served as an adviser to Lloyd George in the Ministry of Munitions.

The two other Whisky Barons came from families that were relatively affluent. The Haig family had been distilling in the Lowlands of Scotland for as long as anybody, and in 1665 one of them was summoned to appear before the Kirk Sessions for having distilled on a Sunday. In the nineteenth century the Haigs were one of the largest distilling companies in Scotland, producing huge quantities of spirit, mainly for rectifying into gin. The company was one of the first to use the patent still, and when they began producing blended whisky they too started to buy malt whisky distilleries.

By the beginning of the First World War John Haig's Gold Label and Dimple Haig blends were well established in export markets. The war hit the whisky trade badly. When it started, Lloyd George took the view that all distilling and the brewing of beer should be stopped and prohibition introduced. He claimed that drunkenness among munition workers was hindering production and resulting in the output of large quantities of sub-standard guns and shells. In fact, as historians were later able to show, the poor performance of the munition industry was due to bad management and inadequate training of inexperienced workers.

Only after difficult negotiations were leaders of the trade able to make him change his mind by pointing out the value of many by-products of distilling, particularly yeast. Distilling continued, but was restricted to save cereals because of the threats to imports by submarines, and some distillers agreed to switch to making acetone for industrial purposes. In addition, an Act of Parliament was passed stipulating that all whisky must be matured for a minimum of two years, a period which was shortly extended to three.

We have become so accustomed to Scotch Whisky as a smooth, mellow drink that it is not always realised that before this Act was passed there was no compulsion to mature whisky. Most malt whisky was matured simply because maturation made it a better and more acceptable drink, but with the advent of the patent still, volume became more important than quality and large quantities of cheap, immature whisky taken virtually straight off the still appeared on the market. The 1910 Royal Commission, by refusing to recommend a minimum period of maturation, was seen to be condoning this. It was on the recommendation of James Stevenson, a director of John Walker and Sons who had also been recruited to advise the government, that the Immature Spirits Act was introduced. With hindsight we can see that this legislation, long overdue, was vital to the future of Scotch Whisky as an international drink. One could argue that reputable distillers and blenders would in any case have continued to market their whisky properly matured. No doubt they would have, but sadly, as recent events have shown, there are always people who put profit before quality even if that were to damage the reputation of Scotch Whisky.

Although hit by the war, as most whisky companies were, Haig's also benefited from it, although only indirectly. Douglas Haig, the son of John Haig of Cameronbridge, became Commander-in-Chief of the British army in France. Not surprisingly, the name of Field-Marshal Earl Haig was a great asset to the company as first a director and then its chairman.

The remaining Whisky Baron, though he was never more than a knight, was Peter Mackie. He was fiery as well as restless, and he has been described as 'one-third genius, one-third megalomaniac and one-third eccentric'. Apart from distilling and blending whisky, he was constantly using his energy to plan new ventures. One which might have earned him the label of eccentric was to enter the milling industry and produce a flour which he called B.B.M., the initials standing for Brawn, Bone and Muscle. All the staff of his company were obliged to eat it. One of his better ideas was to give his blend of Scotch the name White Horse after an Edinburgh inn, and another was to introduce screw caps for his bottles rather than corks, before any of his rivals thought of them.

The Distillers Company had not been idle, watching the expansion and success of these five companies. It had itself been buying malt whisky distilleries. When it had been originally formed, it had agreed that it would not distribute whisky in the United Kingdom, but it was exporting blended Scotch under its own label. It was also supplying whisky to the major blenders and giving them, particularly Dewar's, substantial credit.

Throughout this period the whisky trade was cyclical, periods of boom being followed by depression, caused either by over-production or increases in Excise Duty. The Distillers Company was able, either on its own or acting with one of the major blenders, to take over insolvent companies, some of which had a significant export business.

Its ultimate goal was amalgamation: to bring the most successful blending houses – Dewar's, Buchanan's, Walker's, Haig's and White Horse – into a single fully integrated company with the Distillers Company. The First World War, with its restrictions on distilling, postponed the realisation of this plan, but when peace returned, it was pursued relentlessly by William Ross, the Managing Director of the D.C.L., who patiently undertook the long negotiations. Haig's were the first to agree to amalgamation in 1919 and Walker's, Buchanan's and Dewar's finally entered the combine in 1925. Two years later the D.C.L. acquired control of White Horse.

A merger of those proportions would not be allowed today. In both production and sale, the new company controlled at least sixty per cent of Scotland's whisky industry; that was the recognised proportion, and it might well have been higher. Calculations of that type are difficult if not impossible, because whisky companies do not publish figures of their sales or production. Overall figures for the industry are available from official sources and any whisky firm can, by comparing its own figures, calculate the share it holds. They are all understandably coy about revealing that figure.

This final step in the creation of an amalgamated Distillers Company Limited was a momentous event for the Scotch Whisky business. For the next half-century the company dominated the trade. Not only was it able to dictate prices in both the home and export markets, but it dominated industry policy as well. For much of the time it had a virtual monopoly of grain whisky and could, if it wished, have withheld supplies from any blending company which it believed not to be acting in the interests of the trade as a whole. Whether this was morally right is a matter of opinion, but no one can deny that the formation of the D.C.L. brought a period of stability to the whisky trade which made possible its remarkable expansion after the Second World War.

Because of its corporate size, embracing not only whisky but the production of gin, vodka and for some years pharmaceuticals, the company also had considerable influence with the government. It used this for the interests of the industry as a whole, but not even it was able to deflect Whitehall from its blinkered and illogical taxation policy. Writing in the 1950s, an author commented that the D.C.L.'s greatest contribution to the whisky trade had been to restrain the over-production which had bedevilled it for the past hundred years. As events were to prove, dramatically, and for the industry painfully, he was wrong, but that again is another story.

In her day Bessie Campbell may have been the only woman to be running a distillery, but she was not the only woman of distinction in the whisky business. Ethel Robertson was one of three sisters, grand-daughters of W.A. Robertson, a founding partner of the Glasgow firm of whisky blenders, Robertson and Baxter. I first met her at a hotel in Forres, near Elgin, where the Malt Distillers of Scotland were holding their Annual General Meeting. Members of the Association had gathered at the hotel on the evening prior to the meeting and were dining at the hotel. Dinner was almost over, which means at about seven-thirty at a Scottish country hotel, when Ethel Robertson hurried in and sat down at the vacant place beside me.

'Thank goodness!' she exclaimed. 'I thought we were going to miss dinner. John had to drive like a demon to get here in time.'

She explained that she and John Macphail, a fellow director of Robertson and Baxter, had been visiting one of the company's distilleries in Rothes. John had a powerful car at the time, I believe it was a Bristol, and I could picture this charming, elderly spinster being paralysed with fear as he took corners on two wheels on the narrow, twisting roads.

During dinner Miss Robertson, who I discovered was known to her friends as Babs, suggested that the next time I was in Glasgow I should go and lunch at the company's offices in West Nile Street. A few weeks later, when I took up her invitation and arrived at the offices, I realised how fortunate I had been in my choice of date, for not only Babs but her two sisters, Agnes and Elspeth, were there. They were all directors of the Robertson Trust, which gives substantial sums to charity as well as sponsoring research at academic institutions, and the Trust was meeting that day in Glasgow.

At the end of a delightful family-style lunch, in which Babs carved the roast, she asked me my plans for the afternoon. When I told her I would be flying to London, she insisted on having me driven to the airport in one of the company's cars. So after a glass of Highland Park single malt whisky with my coffee, I went down to the garage where a chauffeur in a Jaguar was waiting. I was sitting in the car and the chauffeur had started the engine, when suddenly he paused. From behind us came the throaty growl of a powerful sports car engine.

'We had better wait and let Miss Ethel out first, sir,' the chauffeur said.

We watched as a long, low Aston Martin nosed out from behind us. As she drove past and up the ramp leading to the street, Babs waved to me. On our way to the airport I learnt that this elderly lady, for whom I had felt so sorry back in Forres, had a passion for fast cars. She would 'commute' three times a week in her Aston Martin right across Scotland from their home at Berwick-on-Tweed where the three sisters had a farm, kennels and a string of racehorses.

'I can tell you one thing,' the chauffeur said. 'If I ever see her on the road I move aside to let her pass. She never drives at less than ninety.'

They say that all the police in Scotland knew her and her

Aston Martin, but would tactfully look the other way when they saw her approach. The only time she was ever stopped by a policeman was when she set out from West Nile Street with her handbag on the roof of the car.

Ethel Robertson remained on the board of Robertson and Baxter until her death in 1985. She was immensely popular in the whisky business, admired for her knowledge and ability and loved for her charm and kindness.

Glasgow has always been linked with whisky. At the end of the Industrial Revolution it was one of the major cities of the British Empire, its prosperity depending largely on ship-building, steel and heavy engineering. When these industries went into decline, internationally as well as in Scotland, Glasgow declined too. The Clyde and large areas of the city were slowly devastated; Sauchiehall Street, once brilliantly alive, was taken over by Chinese and Indian take-away restaurants – 'carry outs' as we call them in Scotland – and the large Victorian homes of wealthy iron-masters were converted into bed-sitters. Emptying the working-class areas into the new towns of Cumbernauld and East Kilbride only exacerbated the problem.

Now Glasgow is recovering. Spectacular new shopping precincts have been built, the city's splendid art galleries have been refurbished or rehoused. Porsches and BMWs, once regarded as the prerogative of London yuppies, can be seen speeding from Blytheswood Square down the steep hills, switchbacking over the intersecting streets as police cars do in San Francisco movies. I have always felt at home in San Francisco, thinking of it as a kind of poor man's Glasgow.

Throughout the bad years, the whisky trade never lost faith in Glasgow, because so many of its roots are there. It was a Glasgow firm, W.P. Lowrie, which gave Buchanan his start, and Buchanan himself, although operating out of

London, thought it important to have an office in the city. Later his Black and White whisky was bottled there.

At the time when Buchanan, Dewar and Walker were laying the foundations of what was to become an immense export business for Scotch Whisky, a number of firms in Scotland were concentrating their attention on selling their whisky at home. One of the earliest to do this was William Teacher and Sons, which has always held a leading position in the home market for Scotch with its Highland Cream blend. William Teacher entered the wine and spirit trade in 1834, when he went to work in his mother-in-law's small shop in the Anderston district of Glasgow. Although one could call it a wine and spirit business, it was in fact a licensed grocer. Licensed grocers were for many years a uniquely Scottish institution. Nothing similar existed in England at that time, although in today's more liberal climate of opinion almost any shop in England seems able to sell wine and beer, as well as spirits. Another unique institution in Scotland which, as far as one can tell, was started by William Teacher was the 'dram shop'.

Contemporary photographs show that they were very different from the pubs of today. Austere and functional, they allowed the customer to buy a dram of whisky for threepence and drink it there, but they made no concessions to his comfort or sociability. Smoking was not allowed, customers could not treat other people to drinks and decorum was strictly maintained. Anyone drinking too much or behaving rowdily was made to leave, so much so that the licensing magistrates even commended Teacher's for their efforts to encourage temperance. This does not appear to have inhibited the drinkers of Glasgow and within a relatively short time Teacher's had eighteen dram shops in different parts of the city. Today the company, with its head office in the main shopping centre, is still a part of the Glasgow scene and actively supports its civic and cultural life, music and Scottish opera in particular.

Another Glasgow firm was formed when James Whyte and Charles Mackay went into partnership. It is not criticism of the company to say that in some ways it has been a late developer. In 1960 it merged with Dalmore distillery and since then its growth has been remarkable. Not only has it acquired two more malt whisky distilleries, but more recently ten brands of blended Scotch well-known in the United Kingdom market, making it now one of the leaders in the home trade.

Whyte and Mackay have an interesting 'double marriage' technique which they use with their blended whisky. Many companies, though not all, after blending their malts and grains together, return the blend to casks for a further period of marrying. Whyte and Mackay first vat or blend together the thirty-five different malts which they use and then return them to sherry wood butts to marry for a period of eight months. The single grain whiskies are then added and the blend once more returned to casks to marry for a further several months. As far as I know, it is the only company to use this technique, which it believes is essential to obtain a blended Scotch of the finest quality.

A number of other Scotch Whisky companies, although not based in Glasgow, have their whisky blended and bottled just outside the city. One reason for this is economy. Modern bottling halls require a large acreage of land, and this is less expensive in outlying districts. Another reason is the memory of the notorious Cheapside fire of 1960, when a whisky warehouse caught fire and nineteen people were killed. Memories of disaster die slowly and the fear of a repetition of that fire still lingers. William Grant and Sons, although it bottles its single malt whisky in Dufftown at the distillery and is the only company that does so, has a bottling hall for its blended whisky at Paisley. Seagram Distillers also bottles its de luxe blend Chivas Regal at Paisley, and Justerini and Brooks bottles J. and B. Rare a little further out of Glasgow at Dumbarton. Cutty Sark is bottled at Drumchapel. Taking all this together, the whisky industry has a substantial investment in the city and this is very unlikely to change.

The rivalry between Glasgow and Edinburgh causes amusement south of the border. The English find it hard to believe, suspecting that it might be no more than a pretence, like the reputation the Scots have given themselves for meanness. Those who live or work with people from both cities know that the antipathy is real enough and that although it finds expression in rivalries, some quite petty, the feeling is much deeper than mere envy. What is astonishing is that two cities only forty minutes' drive apart should be so different. The reasons are as much ethnic as historical or cultural. Immigration up the Clyde and into Glasgow by the Irish has been followed in more recent times by a more modest invasion of Italians, and Jews have always felt more at home there than in Edinburgh. Jack House, an eminent Glasgow journalist, summed up the cultural differences by remarking that in Edinburgh breeding is equated with good form, while in Glasgow breeding is equated with good fun.

Edinburgh is the centre of administration, law and medicine in Scotland and also the capital. One has the feeling that Glaswegians resent this. It is the resentment of a man who has worked hard for everything he has achieved and sees an accolade awarded to what he believes to be a less worthy, even though more gifted, rival. Edinburgh people are aware of this feeling, even though they pretend to treat it with disdain.

When it was announced that Glasgow was to be European

City of Culture for 1990, a whisky man I know asked, 'Which culture? Yeast or penicillin?'

Besides being the capital, Edinburgh is an outstandingly beautiful city. They used to call it 'The Athens of the North', a comparison which today is scarcely flattering, for unlike Athens, Edinburgh has kept not only its historic monuments but much of its beauty. Robert Louis Stevenson described it as a 'profusion of eccentricities, this dream in living masonry and rock'. The castle stands on its rock, brooding it seems over the city's turbulent history. From it one can look down on the elegance of the eighteenth-century New Town, with its squares and crescents planned by half a dozen architects, including Robert Adam.

Of course, not all the charm of Edinburgh has escaped unsullied. The Royal Mile which leads down from the castle to Holyrood House, the palace of the sovereign when in Edinburgh, has its share of pizza houses and tourist shops. From Deacon Brodie's, the pub named after Edinburgh's most notorious criminal, a pillar of the church by day and a burglar by night who was hanged in 1788, canned music blares out, and I have been told that it does not even have a decent selection of single malts on display. But these are small blemishes on a street which offers a journey through history.

Even though the Guild of Surgeon Barbers was given a monopoly of selling whisky as long ago as 1505, Edinburgh has never had as close an affinity with Scotch Whisky as Glasgow has. No doubt Glaswegians would say that this is just evidence of the conceit of Edinburgh folk who think distilling is beneath them. A more plausible explanation is that Glasgow, with its docks, was the natural place for an industry which wished to ship most of its production overseas. For this reason, too, such whisky firms as exist in the east have mainly been concentrated in Leith. This ancient port had been of commercial importance since the fifteenth century, even though in recent times its harbour and docks offer a sad reminder of the decline in the world's shipping trade. Now it is beginning to acquire a reputation for being trendy, with modern town houses, apartments, over-priced restaurants and wine bars springing up along the waterfront.

Today one finds two major whisky companies in Leith. Macdonald and Muir, the owners of Glenmorangie and Glen Moray distilleries, are also whisky blenders, with Highland Queen as their main brand. Invergordon Distillers have their premises on part of what was once Leith Links, one of the earliest golf courses. It had only five holes but also the distinction that the first rules of golf were drawn up there in 1728. There were a mere thirteen rules, and many players today, baffled by the complexity of the rules and their susceptibility to different interpretations, often feel it would have been better to have left them at thirteen. The real purist would say that you need only one rule, 'Play the ball where it lies.'

The 'playing of the Gowff on the Links at Leithe' goes back much earlier than the drawing up of rules, for James IV of Scotland played there in 1505. A match of special, but macabre, interest was that played in 1724 between the Honourable Alexander Elphinstone, brother of Lord Balmerino, and Captain John Porteous of the Edinburgh City guard. We do not know who won the match, played for a stake of twenty guineas, but Porteous lost his life not long afterwards. As Captain of the City Guard, he was supervising the execution of a whisky smuggler when the mob which had gathered to watch became unruly and threatened to rescue the prisoner. Anyway, that was what Porteous thought, and he ordered his soldiers to fire on the people. Some were killed, and Porteous was arrested and imprisoned. When they heard a rumour that he was to be released, the mob broke into the prison and lynched him.

The investment of the whisky industry in and around Edinburgh has declined in recent years. The Distillers Company used to have its head office there in Torphichen Street, an austere building, though that was not the reason why directors of its subsidiary companies used to call it, and only partly in jest, the Kremlin. The company, now the United Distillers Group, still has its Scottish office in Edinburgh, but the offices which a number of its smaller companies had in the city, including for example Macdonald Greenlees, blenders of Old Parr, and J. and G. Stewart of Leith, no longer exist.

The bottling halls in and around Edinburgh are not as large as those in the Glasgow area, but they still provide useful and continuing employment. Both Macdonald and Muir and Invergordon Distillers bottle in Leith, and Seagram Distillers have a bottling hall almost opposite the Grounds where the Highland Show is held each year. Both The Glenlivet and Glen Grant single malt whiskies are bottled there, and not far away in Broxburn Arthur Bell's and Sons of Perth have a large modern hall, which was opened in 1971. Peter Russell's Isle of Skye blend is also bottled in Broxburn. Sadly the bond and bottling halls of William Sanderson, which were a landmark overlooking the Firth of Forth at South Queensferry, and where Vat 69 used to be bottled, are no longer in use.

The former premises of J. and G. Stewart in The Vaults at Leith still have a whisky connection. Part of them are now occupied by the Malt Whisky Society, an organisation created to exploit the growing interest in Scotch single malt whiskies. Visitors to the centre can sample a wide selection of single malts, and members have the opportunity to buy selected malts bottled by the society, very often at high strengths. In another part of The Vaults there is a restaurant, the Vintner's Rooms, which can be strongly recommended both for the excellence of its cuisine and its ambience.

J. and G. Stewart was the company which absorbed Andrew Usher's firm, and Usher has left his own memorial in Edinburgh, the Usher Hall. For almost as long as anyone can remember there has been talk in Edinburgh of building a new opera house to replace the Usher Hall, whose acoustics experts say leave much to be desired. The City Fathers have always found a reason for not agreeing to this and I used to wonder whether this might be because of a sentimental wish to respect Usher's memory by leaving with his concert hall the distinction of hosting all the main events of the city's famous Festival. I should have known better. Rumour has it now that they have at last decided to build an opera house. And the reason? Because they heard that Glasgow has built a new theatre.

Returning to history, it is a curious fact that the licensed grocers or wine merchants who first saw the potential for blended Scotch Whisky were not in either Edinburgh or Glasgow. John Walker and Sons had their business in Kilmarnock, Buchanan began trading in London and John Dewar came from Perth. Dewar's were only one of the wine merchants in Perth to enter the blending trade, the others being Matthew Gloag and Sons and Arthur Bell and Sons. The reasons for this may be partly historical. The 'Fair City', as Perth has been called, was once the ancient capital of Scotland and it was at the Palace of Scone, just outside the city, that the Kings of Scotland were crowned until the coronation stone was looted by Edward I and taken to Westminster.

A more important reason for Perth's role in the development of blending was geographical. Until after Culloden and the subjugation of the Highlands it was not only the gateway north but the nearest and largest market for the whisky smugglers. To this extent it was already a whisky town well before blending began.

Matthew Gloag, born in 1797, started work in the service of the Earl of Mansfield in Scone Palace and later became butler in the home of the Sheriff-Clerk of Perthshire, who also owned Glenalmond Lodge on a large estate to the west of the city. One of his duties was to send instructions to Glenalmond for disposing of the game shot on the estate. In a letter which still exists he gave instructions for the despatch of grouse to various households in Edinburgh and Perth, adding 'one bird and a very small one to yourselves'. One can assume that it was this letter which gave a later Matthew Gloag the inspiration to market a blend of Scotch Whisky under the name The Famous Grouse.

Long before that, though, the business of Gloag's the wine merchants was well established, and in 1842 he was invited to supply the wines for a banquet given in Perth for Queen Victoria on her first visit to Scotland. The firm's wine lists from the 1860s show clearly that whisky as a drink still did not rank very highly among the wealthy. On it Glenlivet and other malt whiskies are priced between fifteen and eighteen shillings for a dozen bottles, cheaper even than rum and only half the price of cognac. Ports range from thirty and sixty shillings a dozen, while first-growth wines from Bordeaux command upwards of seventy shillings a dozen. The thought of being able to buy a bottle of Glenlivet for between seven or eight pence in today's currency must stir the imagination of any whisky lover, but a lot of malts and grains have flowed along the blending troughs since those days.

7

The Golden Years

When the *Titanic* sank in 1912 and more than fifteen hundred
people were drowned, an Aberdeen newspaper carried a front
page headline: ABERDEEN MAN LOST AT SEA. Even today
Scotland's leading newspapers will devote most of their front
pages to the performance of the country's football team in an
international match at Hampden Park, while relegating the
assassination of a world political leader to a few inconspicuous paragraphs.

We Scots are a parochial race. We love our roots with a
fierce, proud passion and treat our English neighbours with a
polite condescension for living in so underprivileged a

country. So how is it that only five million Scots live in Scotland, while an estimated fifty million or more have made their homes in other, more distant, parts of the world?

Dr Samuel Johnson once remarked that 'the noblest prospect' which a Scotsman sees is the road to England. Self-opinionated cynic he may have been, but one can see the accuracy of his assessment, that is, if one is talking only of economic prospects. England can offer nothing in culture, learning or morality, let alone beauty that will surpass Scotland. The sad truth is that it is the Scots and not the English who are economically underprivileged. That is why so many able and ambitious young men take the high road to the south and from there move on around the world. A poor country with few natural resources, Scotland cannot offer the career opportunities to match the excellence of a public education that is the best in Britain, possibly in the world. That is why a ludicrously disproportionate number of London's major businesses and financial institutions are run by Scotsmen.

The Scotsman's readiness to leave his native land, to travel and to settle so easily almost anywhere in the world has been an enormous asset to the Scotch Whisky business. Tom Dewar and the others who wished to sell their brands of whisky abroad found their first markets among expatriate Scots in Australia, New Zealand, South Africa and the other countries of the British Commonwealth. The wanderlust of the Scots was an asset in another way, for it meant that there was never any shortage of able young men ready to travel the world and sell whisky.

Some politician, I forget who it was but I doubt whether he ever sold so much as a hairpin, once said that exporting was fun. No one could deny that the life of a whisky salesman has its enjoyable aspects, but to leave home and family and set out on trips abroad lasting anything from six weeks to six months calls for a special kind of dedication to one's work. Contrary to what some journalists and most politicians appear to believe, Scotch Whisky does not sell itself. Even in the golden years, when demand was increasing in almost every part of the world, there was always the competition of rival brands to face.

The Dewars, Buchanans and Walkers had made good progress in raising the international status of Scotch, when the trade suffered a sudden reverse as a result of two events which few would have foreseen. The first was the outbreak of war in 1914, bringing restrictions on distilling and a near paralysis of shipping because of submarine warfare. The second, which at first, it seemed, would mean an end to the rapidly expanding sales of Scotch in the United States, was Prohibition.

Two whisky companies which suffered particularly were based in London. Both had been established wine merchants for more than two centuries, but at that time they were only making their first moves to enter the whisky export business.

A young Italian from Bologna, Giuseppi Justerini, had come to London in 1749, bringing with him three recipes from his uncle, a distiller who had specialised in compounding liqueurs. Giuseppi had come, not in search of a fortune, but to follow an opera singer, Margherita, with whom he was in love and who had been given a contract to sing in London. He was fortunate enough through contacts in the theatrical world to be introduced to George Johnson, who was looking for a profitable investment for his money and congenial employment for himself. And that was how the firm of Johnson and Justerini came into existence.

History has not recorded whether Justerini ever married his opera singer, but we know he had made enough money at the end of twenty years to retire from business and return to Italy. The wine merchants' firm continued to sell its products in the fashionable part of London around Pall Mall, run first by Johnson and later by his heirs until 1831 when the Johnsons sold it to an Alfred Brooks. For a reason that he never explained and no one else understood, Brooks decided to drop the name of Johnson but to keep the Justerini and so the new firm became Justerini and Brooks.

No one knows how the firm developed to sell its brand of blended Scotch, J. and B. Rare, for its records of that period were destroyed, but it had the whisky ready to ship to America when Prohibition ended. In fact even before repeal Eddie Tatham, one of the directors, went to the States to assess the prospects for its success. He may have been a little too enthusiastic, for he took samples of the blend with him and was unlucky enough to be caught with them and arrested in New York on Grand Central Station. Fortunately he had friends influential enough to arrange for his release.

Just around the corner from Pall Mall in St James's Street, another firm of wine merchants have occupied the same premises since 1699. Originally the business was described as that of 'Italian Warehousemen', a term for grocers who also sold spices, tobacco, snuff, tea and coffee. Exactly when William Pickering, who started the firm, began selling wines and spirits as well is not known, but his daughter married a John Berry from Exeter who was a wine merchant. The firm remained in the sole ownership of the Berry family until after the First World War, when Hugh Rudd came to join it as a partner. Berry Brothers and Rudd are still one of the best known wine merchants in Britain and they still occupy the original shop at Number 3, St James's Street.

For more than two hundred years its customers have included royalty, the nobility, prime ministers, bankers, writers, actors and anyone else with the taste to buy fine wines and the money to pay for them. The interior of the shop, with its oak panelling, antique writing tables, old prints and even older ledgers, seems scarcely to have changed at all over the centuries. Many customers would come there simply to be weighed on its giant scales. The weights of Pitt, Byron, Beau Brummell, Melba and, from more recent times, Gertrude Lawrence, Lord Olivier and 'Rab' Butler, as well as scores of other celebrities, are recorded in the 'weighing' book.

Cutty Sark, the firm's brand of Scotch Whisky, dates back to 1923, when its label with the sketch of the famous sailing ship was designed. Besides being the name of the tea clipper, Cutty Sark was one of the characters in Burns's poem 'Tam o'Shanter'.

Cutty Sark and J. and B. Rare have two things in common. For both whiskies the blends were created by Charles Julian, in his day a well-known blender and whisky broker. Unlike many whiskies, neither blend has any caramel added and for this reason both are unusually pale in colour. Both quickly became international brands and both came to have a special appeal to Americans. Perhaps it was because of their lightness in flavour as well as colour, which may be equated by health-conscious Americans with a lower calorie content. On the other hand, it may simply have been that both companies chose outstandingly good importers to distribute their whisky in the States. Whatever the reason, when the popularity of Scotch was at its peak there, J. and B. Rare and Cutty Sark led the way in sales.

J. and B. Rare is also a brand leader in Italy. Obviously Giuseppi Justerini cannot be given the credit for this, as one doubts whether anyone in Italy would even have heard of whisky in his day. Is it too fanciful though to imagine that there may be something in the pedigree of J. and B. Rare, some distantly Italianate strain, which accounts for its success? And, if one carries the fancy a little further, it might also be that Italiante strain which helped raise J. and B. Rare to stardom in the States. The concierge of a hotel in Venice, Signor Polombo, a man of immense dignity and distinction, once gave me a record of a song called 'Venezia, No!', which he had composed. Few people in Italy had even heard the song, but in America it had been in the top ten tunes and had made Signor Polombo a millionaire. One could almost see homesick Italians in Brooklyn weeping into their J. and B. Rare whisky as they listened to it.

In 1920 Larry Fay, a poorly paid New York taxi driver, struck lucky twice. First he had a winning bet at the race-track on a 100 to 1 outsider and he used the winnings to buy his own cab. Soon afterwards he was flagged down by a man who wanted to be driven to Montreal, a journey of almost four hundred miles. In Montreal, after dropping his fare, Fay noticed that good Scotch Whisky was priced at ten dollars a case. He bought two cases, smuggled them over the border and sold them in New York for two hundred dollars.

He began crossing over into Canada as often as he could, and soon he was wealthy enough to have a fleet of cabs. From there he moved into protection rackets and speakeasies. The El Fey club provided under-the-table booze and extravagant entertainment, including a jazz band and a girl who danced covered only with a python. Fay was said to have made seven hundred thousand dollars out of the club in its first year. His luck ran out when he was shot four times in the stomach by a disgruntled employee from one of his speakeasies. The name of the racehorse which had given him the entree to this brief acquaintance with high life was 'Scotch Verdict'.

By the time Fay died, the smuggling of Scotch from Canada into the States had become a big and profitable business. Enterprising Canadians had set up warehouses near the border to which bootleggers could race through the 'whisky gap' and load up their specially equipped cars. The Studebaker Whisky Six, with reinforced springs, could carry at least forty cases of Scotch, once its upholstery had been removed. One Canadian supplier had even built a garage near his warehouse, where the cars could be serviced before starting on their return journey.

The main threat to a successful run was neither the Canadian customs nor the Federal agents on the other side of the border, both of whom took a tolerant view of these little misdemeanours or had been bribed to ignore them. The real danger was of being hijacked by rival bootleggers after crossing the border, and standard equipment on the Whisky Six included bullet-proof petrol tanks and a length of chain which, when dragged behind the car on dirt roads, blinded pursuing drivers.

Smuggling by road across the border was only one of many ways in which Scotch was supplied to Americans during their long, enforced, thirst. A former World War One flying ace even ran a regular night airline service carrying whisky between southern Ontario and small airports in Michigan. Al Capone's brother had a fleet of twenty planes doing the same thing, and other bootleggers were shipping Scotch in small boats across the Detroit River from Windsor, Ontario.

All this was possible because it was condoned by the Canadian government, which took the view that exporting liquor was legal and if the liquor was exported to a country where importing it was illegal, that was not Canada's responsibility. The advocacy of this Jesuitical argument may not have been unconnected with the fact that the exports of liquor were good for Canada's trade balance. In the first year of Prohibition alone exports of liquor to the United States were worth more than a hundred million dollars.

The amount of Scotch shipped into the States through Canada was, if one may use the expression, small beer compared with the quantity which went in by sea. The most favoured area for this smuggling was between Boston and Atlantic City, a stretch which came to be known as 'Rum Row'. There, every day a fleet of fifty ships or more, fishing schooners, steam yachts and a few small cargo vessels, could be seen sailing up and down, offering cargoes of Scotch, champagne and brandy to bootleggers, who came out in fast boats to buy it. Often the ships would hang signs over their sides announcing their prices, and some were even brazen enough to hoist signal pennants with the message 'Come and Get It'.

Much of the Scotch came from the Bahamas, where companies established depots from which their whisky could be shipped to Rum Row. Nassau, lazy and sun-drenched, with a few streets of dilapidated wooden buildings and not much more except banana groves, was transformed into a boom town, full of fast-talking, fast-drinking characters who were there to make deals in the Scotch which lay in bulging warehouses and not above violence and even a little gun-play when they were frustrated.

One character who made a reputation for himself as well as a small niche in history was Bill McCoy, a sailor from Florida. He would load his schooner *Arethusa* with 5,000 cases of Scotch in Nassau and sail it to Rum Row. By the time he entered the business, rum-running into the States was growing so fast that suppliers and distillers had became greedy and were shipping out brandy, rum and whisky of the

165

poorest quality. McCoy shrewdly realised that a reputation for integrity might be an asset, and he decided he would refuse to carry anything except good quality liquor, mainly Scotch Whisky. So as he sailed up and down Rum Row, bootleggers would come to the *Arethusa* rather than to other ships, knowing that what he offered would be the genuine article. And that was how the expression 'The Real McCoy', found its way into the dictionaries of the English language.

Bill McCoy became a millionaire, but unlike Larry Fay and scores of others in the smuggling and bootlegging business he did not die a violent death. One day his ship was seized by coastguards, illegally, for he was outside the 3-mile limit. He was arrested, indicted and sentenced to a year in prison. He served his time in comfort, for the jail in New Brunswick was so crowded with Prohibition offenders that the warden allowed him to lodge in a nearby apartment hotel, provided he observed a nine o'clock curfew. When released, he decided that he no longer wished to be involved in a business that had fallen into the control of gangsters, so he took his money and retired to Florida.

In the United States Prohibition led to fourteen years of crime and to the corruption of the police, the judiciary and the administration, the effects of which still linger in American society. Ironically, Scotch Whisky emerged from the turbulent era with its reputation enhanced. Throughout Prohibition Americans could buy liquor almost anywhere they chose; from drugstores, delicatessens, cigar stores, soda fountains and shoeshine parlours, as well as from hotel bellhops. Most of what they were offered in speakeasies was liquor of inferior quality, cheap rye whiskey from Canada and rum from the Caribbean. A good deal of it was illicitly produced alcohol made in the 'alky' stills of the cities, or denatured industrial alcohol. Both could be lethal. 'Black Strap Alky',

'Panther Whiskey' and 'Yack Yack Bourbon' were the names of only a few of the concoctions which killed hundreds of drinkers and left thousands blind.

Americans soon discovered that if they could get hold of a bottle of Scotch, preferably unopened, they would be drinking a spirit of good quality, properly matured and pleasant to taste as well. In this way Scotch was introduced to literally millions of Americans, who before Prohibition would never have even thought of trying it and probably could not have afforded it.

By 1930 politicians had begun to realise that the 'noble experiment', as Prohibition was called back in 1919, had been a disaster. Movements for repeal began to be backed by men of influence like John D. Rockefeller, who had been one of Prohibition's strongest advocates. Opinion polls showed that the vast majority of Americans wanted repeal, and back in Scotland, distillers realised that it was inevitable. Shrewd businessmen in the States began to plan for the bonanza in the drinks trade which would follow. One of them was Joseph Kennedy, father of the late President.

Many stories have been told of how Kennedy exploited repeal. The most common is that, because of his influence in Washington, he knew in advance of the date when the government would repeal the 18th Amendment, or Volstead Act, and began buying large stocks of Scotch Whisky. A refinement of this tale is that he had actually bought them and had ships loaded with Scotch waiting outside New York harbour, ready to sail in as soon as drinking became legal again. Whatever the truth, and it may lie somewhere between the two stories, it is good to know that the fortune of the family which prided itself on its Irish roots was founded not on Irish Whiskey but on Scotch.

The repeal of Prohibition did not lead immediately to a

surge in the demand for Scotch in the States. The effects of the Depression in the early 1930s and the Wall Street Crash were exacerbated by increased import duties. When these duties were halved in 1935, shipments to the States immediately began to increase. Such was the interest shown in Scotch that large numbers of American firms sent representatives to Scotland, looking for exclusive agencies as distributors of leading brands. At the same time American distilling companies began investing in the Scotch business by buying distilleries in Scotland.

The outbreak of war in 1939 put an immediate end to expansion. Distilling was at first restricted and then stopped altogether for a time, as the government refused to make any cereals available. It was only resumed when the prospects of victory in the war seemed certain. Even then, supplies of grain were made available only on the understanding that the new whisky produced was intended for sale overseas. The government had recognised that Scotch Whisky represented an enormous potential for the country's post-war economy. Winston Churchill wrote:

On no account reduce the barley for whisky. This takes years to mature and is an invaluable export and dollar producer. Having regard to all our other difficulties about export, it would be most improvident not to preserve this characteristic British element of ascendancy.

In the golden years that followed, Scotch Whisky proved that Churchill's confidence in it had not been misplaced. The expansion in world sales over the next three decades was extraordinary and nothing like it had ever been seen in the long history of drink and drinking. Shipments of Scotch to overseas markets doubled in less than ten years, doubled again in the following seven and doubled yet again in the next six years. Bare figures do not do justice to what was a social phenomenon. Suddenly everyone seemed to be drinking Scotch. To serve it at diplomatic receptions and soirées in embassies, wherever they might be, became obligatory. It replaced champagne as the fashionable drink in nightclubs and very soon was easily the largest selling item in duty-free stores on every ship and at every airport.

How did this happen? A number of explanations have been advanced, and even in the whisky trade almost everyone has his own theory. The quickest growth in sales was in the United States and it has been suggested that the Second World War was itself partly responsible for this. Hundreds of thousands of American servicemen had crossed the Atlantic to Britain, where they learnt that Scotch more than compensated for the lukewarm beer they were offered in pubs.

The growth in foreign travel from the 1950s onwards also helped, since American tourists coming to Europe for the first time were suspicious of foreign drinks with strange names and gaudy colours. American whiskey would have been hard to find in Europe at that time and everyone would have heard of the name Scotch, even if they had never tasted the drink. If they were film-goers they would certainly have seen it being drunk. Humphrey Bogart, Spencer Tracy and Cary Grant could usually be seen on the screen to be asking for a Scotch, and even Greta Garbo was so carried away that for the first time in a film she spoke, or so the legend says. The immortal words, 'Give me a visky, Baby, and don't be stingy', sound so out of character that one has to suspect that the 'visky' she was demanding could not have been her first. They say that Cutty Sark was Garbo's favourite, while in more recent times Yul Brynner was reluctant to go on location in Italy until he could be guaranteed a supply of The Glenlivet.

The invention by a clever Italian of the Whisky à Gogo club, forerunner of the discotheque, must have given a tremendous boost to the sales of Scotch in Europe. I can recall visiting a club on the Left Bank in Paris in that era, where bottles of Scotch belonging to 'members' were kept locked in glass-fronted cupboards which stretched along the full length of three walls. Each bottle carried a sticky label with the name of the member who had bought it, believing that this would be cheaper than buying Scotch by the glass. In theory it was, for the bar price of a glass was unbelievable, but in reality it was a gentle form of confidence trick. Having invested in a bottle, the member would visit the club more often than he normally would and, while there, he would also drink more than usual.

On the evening of my visit I calculated that there were at least four hundred bottles in the cupboards, mostly of Johnnie Walker Black Label or Chivas Regal and all already paid for. All one can say is that it represented a very nice capital sum which the owners could use to run the business. It has never been the distillers who make the most money out of Scotch.

Regine's was the most exclusive night spot in Paris in those days. If one could find a way of getting admitted – tipping the doorman was not usually enough – one would find film stars and members of the government mingling with royalty from Monaco. Almost without exception everyone would be drinking Scotch, even though several of the younger *vedettes* of stage or screen would be drinking theirs mixed with Coca-Cola.

Prohibition, the war and the spread of tourism may all have helped to create the climate in which Scotch could flourish and the movies, the novels of Françoise Sagan and discotheques provided a form of free advertising to promote its reputation. This should not in any way detract from the speed and skill with which the whisky trade saw and accepted the opportunities which faced it. Companies formed networks of distribution in countries all over the world to handle sales of their brands.

In most cases this involved giving a local agent the exclusive right to distribute a brand of Scotch in a country or, in the case of large countries, a territory. These agents would usually be companies which handled several different types of alcoholic drinks, domestic as well as imported. In their portfolios they would probably have a brand of champagne, a port, a sherry and the wines of reputable shippers in France, Germany and Italy. A company's sales force, when it went on the road, would be seeking orders for a number of different products which, of course, made the selling operation more economic.

Only by using sole distributors could smaller whisky companies market their brands in many different countries. One could find literally scores of Scotches scarcely known in Scotland on sale in Europe, North and South America and the Far East. In this way some relatively minor brands found a niche for themselves and a very profitable one in certain export markets. Old Parr, a de luxe brand named, for some reason, after a Cornishman who lived to be one hundred and fifty-two, is one of the top sellers in Japan. Doctor's Special, a stable companion to Ballantine's, is a favourite in Sweden, though whether this is a reflection of the Swedes' neurotic obsession with their health one cannot say. The sales of Scoresby, which I have never seen available outside the States, are most impressive in California. One can think of many other examples.

At one time some people in the trade felt there were too many brands of Scotch available and that this was only

171

causing confusion in the minds of the consumer. A contrary view was that every brand on sale increased the exposure of Scotch and helped to make the public more aware of it.

The sales efforts made by distributors were reinforced by advertising and marketing. In spite of the fact that Scotch and other spirits were not allowed to be advertised on television, the annual advertising budgets in the States for the major brands of Scotch ran into several millions of dollars. Advertising was backed by promotions which were sometimes linked to international trade fairs or British Weeks that covered many products other than Scotch. Smaller one-off promotions in stores were commonplace as whisky companies began looking for ways to bring their brands to the attention of consumers.

In the 1950s the main thrust was directed at the United States, where standards of living and disposable income and consumer spending were far higher than in Europe. Before the end of the decade the States were taking more than half of the Scotch shipped out of Scotland. By the 1960s, however, Western Europe had became the fastest growing market, and gradually the main promotional effort was switched to there.

One event I attended was a reception held by Arthur Bell and Sons at the Eiffel Tower in the presence of the British ambassador. The main attraction of the evening, apart from Bell's whisky, was a performance by the Bluebell Girls, who were then appearing in Paris. Unfortunately the evening turned out to be unseasonably chilly. As long as they were dancing the girls were warm enough, but as they mingled with the guests, scantily dressed and at that altitude, they needed a dram to stop them shivering. Even the ambassador could not resist making the obvious pun.

One can almost feel sorry for Bell's, who must have suffered more than most whisky companies from puns. One popular pub story was that of a hunchback who went into a bar in Paris and asked for a Scotch. 'Bells, sir?' the barman enquired. The hunchback's head slumped down on to the bar in despair as he covered his ears with his hands. 'No no! Not the bells!' he groaned. 'Anything but the bells!'

On another occasion, in the Swiss Alps, I can remember being surprised to hear Scottish music, laughter and the unmistakable sound of people enjoying themselves coming from a solitary inn well away from a little skiing resort. John Walker and Sons, I discovered, were promoting their Johnnie Walker whiskies there and the star of the evening was an actor dressed as the dandy in the famous advertisement: 'Johnnie Walker, born 1870 still going strong.' I do not know how the actor was faring, but the party was still going strong in the wee small hours.

An even more spectacular event took place in Cannes during the Annual Film Festival. That year it was the turn of the British film industry to stage a national day and it decided to make it a Scottish day. The government arranged for a regimental pipe band to be there and the Scottish Tourist Board sent over a group of Highland dancers. Scotch Whisky companies agreed to sponsor a banquet in the Casino with haggis and of course whisky. On the day itself a Scottish film was shown, and Scottish actors and actresses appeared. Sean Connery and Deborah Kerr were two whom I remember seeing.

On the morning of the Scottish day I was asked by one of the organisers to tell the Casino's chef how to cook the haggis. Now, haggis has become the subject of weak jokes. Even in highbrow, aloof, Edinburgh one finds tea-towels on sale, decorated with a drawing of a mythical haggis with wings, beak, even horns and a screamingly funny description of the beast's habits and habitat. We Scots find nothing comical about haggis. No one would describe it as a delicacy but, as one might expect in Scotland, it is an economical dish, composed of various unmentionable parts of a sheep's anatomy which might otherwise go to waste, minced up with oatmeal and spices and sewn into the sheep's stomach. Properly cooked it can be very appetising and many a wee Scottish housewife has made her reputation as a cook by providing a first-class haggis for the local Burns Night supper.

I claim no expertise in cooking, and as far as I could tell the only reason I was asked to advise the chef was that I was the only Scot around at that time of the morning. The kitchens of the Casino were out of this world, acres of marble and stainless steel, and lying on one of the tables was a haggis, a real beauty weighing at least eight pounds. Presently the chef arrived, a squat self-assured Corsican. He listened while I told him in my halting French that he must prick the haggis liberally with a needle and then cook it gently in a bain-marie.

Then he sniffed. '*Saucisson*', was all he said before he turned and walked away.

His intonation was a delicate balance between scorn and pity. Who was this Scot who had gone there to tell him, a master chef, how to cook a sausage? I have never before thought of haggis as a sausage, but that of course is precisely what it is, a Scottish sausage. Every country in the world has its national sausage, but perhaps it is only the Scots who could invest theirs with a symbolic, an almost mystical, dignity by having it piped in on ceremonial occasions and an ode recited over it.

The banquet that evening was a *succès fou*. The pipers and the dancers were given an ovation and even the French did not turn up their noses at cock-a-leekie soup and overdone Scottish roast beef. The haggis was rather insipid and so I did what many do and poured a glass of Scotch over it. My neighbour at the table was Bertrand, a gastronomic journalist with an international reputation. He had never tasted haggis before and, when he saw me pour whisky over mine, he did the same.

Curious to know how he rated Scotland's sausage, I asked him for his opinion. He sampled another mouthful before he replied, 'The dish, it is not distinguished, my friend. But the sauce ...,' he pursed up his lips in a kiss of pleasure, 'the sauce is superb.'

In the late 1960s Italy, after a slow start, became one of the best markets for Scotch in Europe and easily the best for single malt whiskies. Much of the credit for this must be given to Armando Giovinetti, who was the importer for Glen Grant, but one cannot help feeling that malt whisky was anyway particularly suited to Italians, who admire style, good taste and luxury. Milan led the way, and very soon one could find a better selection of malt whiskies in its bars than in many of Scotland's pubs; not only in the five-star hotels like Il Principe de Savoia, but in small cafés around Il Duomo.

As in every other country in Europe, Scotch was being energetically promoted. A major and colourful event was the one staged in Venice. The drowsy mediaeval city, which Ruskin found sinful and Proust 'a graveyard of unhappiness', was stirred into gaiety as a pipe band sent the pigeons in the Piazza San Marco spiralling up to the roofs. Everywhere Venetians were introduced to the subtleties of malt whisky; in Harry's Bar on the edge of the lagoon, even in the Danieli Hotel, mausoleum of a thousand honeymoons, where Gabriele d'Annunzio spent his famous 'week of love' with the actress Elenora Duse. Even those two compulsive lovers might have been tempted to leave their four-poster bed by the splendour of the whisky party that was held one night in the Palazzo Ducale. There was piping and dancing in the courtyard, and a buffet for which the chefs had used all their inventiveness, modelling grouse and salmon out of sugar to decorate the tables which were loaded with canapés and almond biscuits.

The Venetians strolled and gossiped in the galleries, drinking the Scotch they were offered with abandon, especially the malt whisky. As the evening passed and their gaiety became even noisier, one could not help wondering whether they were aware of the strength of what they were drinking. Pale in colour and served with plenty of ice-cubes, it might easily have been mistaken by them for one of their native aperitif drinks – Martini Bianco, perhaps. If so, no doubt they realised their mistake when they tried to climb into their gondolas on the way home.

Stung by the success of Scotch in their country, Italian producers of wines and aperitifs fought back by promoting their drinks in Britain. Soon our television screens were enriched with lovely signorinas sipping cool drinks as they lay on the sizzling beaches of Bournemouth. Martini and Rossi, not satisfied with buying a Scotch Whisky company and a distillery, even tried to strike the Scots where it would hurt most by sponsoring a golf tournament. The arrangements for the tournament could not be faulted, except for one tiny misunderstanding. It was at a time when the company was running a television advertising campaign, based on a catchy little jingle which ran: 'Martini – the right one'. A platoon of busty girls was engaged to act as hostesses at the golf. Dressed in minuscule green skirts and white T-shirts, they were to pour drinks for guests, pose for photographs with the golfers and generally make themselves conspicuous. On the first day the tournament nearly did not get off the ground, for when they saw the T-shirts, the girls had gone on strike. What well-endowed girl would wear a T-shirt bearing the caption 'Martini – the right one'? Martini may have learned from that experience. Later they came up with another TV jingle, but as far as one knows no girls have been asked to wear T-shirts carrying the message 'Any time, any place, anywhere.'

On our way to the table he had reserved at le Caprice restaurant, Bill Oatley stopped to chat with a number of people whom I recognised as celebrities of the theatre and cinema. Bill loved the theatre and often lunched at le Caprice, which at that time was a favourite restaurant of stage people. He was then Managing Director of The Distillers Agency, one of the smaller companies in the D.C.L. group, and his office was just round the corner from le Caprice in Pall Mall. When we reached our table, I saw on it an unopened bottle of King George IV, the company's brand of blended whisky. Although not one of the major brands of Scotch, it is excellent, and I have noticed that D.C.L. people often choose it when their own brands are not available.

Presently Bill's other guest at lunch that day arrived. Jack Train was an actor who several years previously had played in a very popular radio show called 'It's That Man Again', ITMA for short, the star of which was Tommy Handley. Jack's part was that of a very bibulous character, Colonel Chinstrap, whose main talent was an ability to interpret almost any remark made to him as an offer of a drink. Over lunch Bill and Jack talked about the show and the actors and actresses who had played in it. We also talked about Scotch.

'I reckon I have sold more whisky than any of Bill's salesmen,' Jack said to me.

I knew he was only being flippant but that he would expect me to ask him to explain the remark, so I did. He told me that every time he had been offered a drink on the show, he would ask for a Scotch. Then he would be asked how he liked his Scotch. The reply was always the same: 'Fifty-fifty. Lots of water.'

Later, when I remembered the banter, I began to reflect on how in fact whisky was sold in the home market. The growing popularity of Scotch abroad was at that time not being matched in the United Kingdom. After the last war, at the request of the government, the whisky trade had agreed to a voluntary restriction of supplies in the home market, so that as much as was available could be used to earn badly needed foreign exchange. This restriction was lifted in 1954, but it was not until 1960 that sales of Scotch in the home market reached their pre-war level. With increased affluence and higher disposable incomes generally, one would have expected home sales to increase. They did, but were held back, as they still are, by constant increases in Excise Duty.

The attitude of the British government to Excise Duties is incomprehensible. Foreigners laugh at us. Who else but the British would tax Scotch Whisky, a domestic product, far more heavily than imported wine? The imagination of White-hall remains firmly embedded in the outmoded belief that beer is the working man's drink and the only vote-catcher. Faced with a crippling Excise Duty, whisky companies have been forced to keep their prices down to an uneconomically low level. As a result there has been little profit to be made out of selling Scotch in the home market. In the 1960s one leading company even withdrew its main brand from the home market and concentrated on exporting it. Calculations had shown that it was making a loss on every bottle of Scotch it sold in Britain.

In these circumstances it is not surprising that little effort has been made over the last three decades to promote Scotch in the home market. Even today it is significant that until recently one of the most popular and widely televised golf tournaments in the UK was sponsored not to promote a brand of Scotch, but by a Japanese whisky company.

When commercial television was introduced in Britain in the 1950s, the producers and importers of all spirits – gin, vodka and rum as well as whisky – entered into a 'gentlemen's agreement' that they would not advertise their products on television. Because profit margins on spirits were so low, they decided that they could not afford to become involved in massive expenditure on TV advertising.

Although one can appreciate the reasons for the agreement, there can be little doubt that it has put spirits, and particularly Scotch Whisky, at a severe commercial disadvantage. Competing drinks such as Campari and Martini have benefitted from their TV advertising, and sales of Scotch in the United Kingdom have never reached their full potential. This is particularly true of sales in England. The English generally know little about Scotch and could have been told of its complexity, character and romantic history in television commercials. As it is, only a very small proportion of the English order their Scotch by brand name, which is why pubs can restrict themselves to stocking one or at most two brands. This is now changing because profit margins have improved, leading to more aggressive marketing by leading brands and the growing interest of consumers in single malt Scotches.

In Scotland, drinkers have a better understanding of their whisky. For this reason and because the majority of Scottish pubs are 'free' houses – that is, not tied to brewers – customers are offered a wider selection of brands. The 'half and half', in other words a half-pint of beer and a small whisky, remains a traditional Scottish way of drinking, in spite of the government's determination to tax Scotch out of the reach of ordinary folk. And one is happy to see that a Scot, having drunk his Scotch, will still hold the glass upside down over the beer until he is certain that not a drop has been wasted. The father of a friend of mine from Stirling carries this admirable habit to its logical extension. Whenever a bottle of Scotch in his home is empty, he stands it neck down in a glass overnight. By next morning he will have collected enough whisky for almost one more dram.

In Bill Oatley's time to be a whisky salesman must have been frustrating. Getting a brand, particularly a new brand, into the pubs was virtually impossible. The same was becoming true of the High Street wine merchants as they were swallowed up by the large brewers. A salesman had few opportunities to show his imagination or flair, to emulate James Buchanan, make flamboyant gestures or ride round London in a pony and trap. It was true that James Buchanan and Company still had their teams of black horses, but they were mainly paraded at agricultural shows and show-jumping events.

In the 1960s and 1970s the representatives of whisky companies – no one likes to be called a salesman now – could be seen in fashionable hotels and restaurants in the West End of London. One could watch them at the bar, having a quiet word with the barman and encouraging him, with an appropriate tip, to pour their whisky whenever a customer ordered a Scotch. The home trade director or manager of the company would lunch or dine with business contacts in the restaurant and have the same encouraging words with the sommelier. At the same time, of course, a bottle of the company's brand would be displayed on the table.

Various devices were used by some companies to secure orders for their brands. One was to offer a bar manager a 'thirteenth' bottle with every case of Scotch he ordered. The incentive was that this bottle could be sold over the bar and the money taken for it need not find its way into the till. This was a policy of desperation and also self-defeating, since it only reduced profit margins still further.

One has to feel sympathy for the representative who has the unrewarding and in many ways monotonous job of trying to sell his company's whisky. Touring bars and restaurants may sound an attractive way of spending one's day, but it soon palls. I was told of one unfortunate who resigned because he could no longer afford the job. His salary was good and of course the bills he incurred in bars and restaurants were all sent direct to the company and settled by it. What he could not afford, or so he claimed, was the amount he was obliged to hand out every day in tips to doormen and cloakroom attendants.

Aruba is a small, arid island, sometimes described as being in the Caribbean, although it is a good deal further to the south than most Caribbean islands. At one time a Dutch colony, it now has autonomous status in the kingdom of Holland. The official language is Dutch, but the island also has its own patois, of which it is very proud. Papiamento is a curious amalgam of several languages adapted from the tongues of the different races who have lived there at one time or another; the indigenous Arawak Indians, the Spanish, Portuguese, English, Dutch, with a few African dialects added for good measure. Almost anyone, whatever his nationality, can recognise a few words when they hear it spoken. For example 'Thank you very much' in Papiamento, 'Masha Danki', is not all that far removed from what one might hear slurred in an English pub as closing time approaches.

The island was 'discovered' in 1499 by the Spaniards, who

wrote it off as 'valueless'. They may have come to regret this peremptory judgment, as gold was discovered there in 1913. When the gold was worked out there came riches from 'black gold', as one of the world's largest refineries was built there to process the product of the nearby oil wells of Venezuela. This bonanza did not last either, for the refinery, which had supplied more than one-third of the oil used by the Allies in the last war, was abruptly closed down in 1985. Now Aruba is rebuilding its economy by exploiting the only asset left to it, its magnificent beaches. A string of hotels is being built along the coast to provide American tourists with inexpensive holidays.

Anyone familiar with the United Kingdom export statistics might wonder whether the Arubans might have found another seam of gold to tap, the liquid gold of Scotch Whisky. Shipments of Scotch to Aruba are currently running at a figure equivalent to more than three million bottles annually. Aruba has a population of about sixty thousand and, taken at face value, these figures would imply that the islanders, men, women and children are each drinking on average about a bottle of Scotch every week, which would make them the heaviest Scotch drinkers in the world.

Obviously they are not drinking that amount. Few Arubans can even afford to drink Scotch. So when I was on the island a couple of years ago, I decided to find out what was happening to it. As a starting point for my enquires I went to see the editor of the island's newspaper. He was a grand fellow, a Dutchman who had fallen in love with the island and was happy to spend the rest of his life there.

At first I thought that I had made a bad choice, for he seemed to have no interest in Scotch. All he wished to talk about was the economy of Aruba and its future. He told me that some three thousand men were working on the construction of hotels, but that the building programme could not last indefinitely. The authorities recognised the potential unemployment that could follow when it stopped, and had opened a hotel and catering school. There the construction workers were being trained in evening classes so that they could fill the new jobs that would be created as the hotels went into operation. It was an ingenious plan, but not without its own problems. Could I imagine how difficult it was to train a builder's labourer to be a barman?

The editor smiled. 'Still, at least he will know how to say "Here's mud in your eye".'

He may have only been showing off his command of English, and with good reason, but having got the joke out of his system, he agreed to talk about whisky. We drove down to the docks where a consignment of Scotch had arrived the previous day. It had been stored in a warehouse by the quay, but would stay there only until the small impost charged by the Aruban government had been paid. One cannot call it import duty, for the whisky does not stay on the island.

The following day the Scotch would be taken from the warehouse and loaded on to small vessels on the other side of the quay. These former fishing boats, I was told, had been fitted with more powerful engines, and they would ship several thousand cases of the Scotch to either Venezuela or Colombia. If they sailed to Venezuela, the cargo would be unloaded on a beach by night. Secrecy was not needed on voyages to Colombia, where the ships could sail into harbour and unload without questions being asked.

Smuggling into Colombia is highly organised and lucrative. In addition to Scotch Whisky, tobacco, imported jeans, computers, television sets and hi-fi equipment, mostly from Japan, are all smuggled into the country and sold openly. Maicao, a town of a hundred thousand people, exists entirely on dealing in smuggled goods.

The smuggling of Scotch is endemic in the South American continent. The reason for it is the restrictions, either in the form of import quotas or punitive import duties, which South American governments impose on Scotch. This may be done to protect a country's balance of payments or to protect domestic drinks industries, or a combination of both motives. Such policies are pursued erratically, restrictions being imposed and then lifted from year to year, without any clear reason for the change. When restrictions are in force, Scotch is smuggled in from neighbouring countries, and at other times the traffic may be reversed. Governments seem ready to ignore the smuggling, even though it must mean a loss of revenue.

Smuggling is by no means confined to Latin America, and Scotch must be the most widely smuggled item in the world. Even though followers of the prophet are not supposed to indulge in alcohol, large consignments used to be shipped into Middle East countries through Lebanon. Given the current political difficultuies in Lebanon, one has a suspicion that another channel is now being used, possibly Cyprus.

If smuggling on a global scale is a measure of the international popularity Scotch has achieved, one of the penalties of that success is the counterfeiting which plagues it. This may take two forms. One is the copying of the bottles and labels of established brands of Scotch Whisky and using them as packaging for locally produced whiskies or other drinks. This type of counterfeiting is relatively rare, because in most countries it is illegal and carries severe penalties.

The second form in its simplest manifestation consists of giving a domestic whisky a name which suggests that it is Scotch, or a label which will imply a Scottish origin. The objective is to deceive consumers into buying the product in the belief that it is genuine Scotch Whisky.

This form of counterfeiting will persist as long as Scotch Whisky enjoys worldwide popularity. If allowed to go unchecked, it could ultimately destroy the reputation of Scotch Whisky and cancel out all the work that has been done to build up its sales abroad. 'Passing off' locally produced 'whiskies' is obviously reprehensible and in most countries legal redress is possible. In some cases the intended fraud can be prevented by opposing the registration of any trademarks which might deceive consumers; in others legal proceedings can be taken against offenders. For several decades now the Scotch Whisky Association and whisky companies have been fighting in the courts and outside them to prevent 'passing off' and in this way protect the geographical description of Scotch Whisky.

Policing the market in many different countries is time-consuming and costly. The distributors and agents of Scotch Whisky companies need to be constantly on the alert to detect the appearance of deceptively labelled local drinks. Bottles of suspect brands must be purchased and sent to Scotland for lawyers to examine and, where thought necessary, for the contents to be analysed. Legal advice is needed before proceedings can be begun and the services of lawyers must be retained in the country where the offence has been committed. Litigation is inevitably a slow process and it may take a long time to obtain a judgment. When practicable the Association seeks not only to stop the sale of the offending brand, but also to secure damages and costs from the defendant.

Offenders are often very ingenious in devising names that clearly suggest Scottish origin but which they can claim do not. One example which appeared some years ago was the name 'Ben Hur'. One can easily imagine the defendant's plea in court. 'Scottish, Your Honour? It's a fine old Roman name!'

One is almost sorry that such ingenuity was in vain and judgment given against the defendant.

The list of countries in which the Scotch Whisky Association or its member companies take legal action is extensive, ranging from the Netherlands and Greece to Ecuador and Surinam. In any one year thirty or more legal cases may be fought in the courts of countries in every continent. The work of protecting the name of Scotch Whisky is never-ending and people in Scotland draw an analogy between it and the painting of the Forth Bridge.

A very high proportion of the brands against which action is taken contain a mixture of Scotch malt whisky and neutral spirit distilled locally, often from molasses. These 'admixtures' can therefore have an appearance and flavour with some resemblance to those of genuine Scotch Whisky. On learning this, people often ask where the admixers get the Scotch malt whisky. The answer is that they can import it in bulk from Scotland.

The export of bulk malt whisky from Scotland is a contentious subject, capable at any time of arousing passionate and acrimonious arguments. On the surface it seems preposterous that, for the sake of a 'fast buck', distillers in Scotland should be ready to provide foreign companies with the wherewithal to produce a spirit – one should not dignify it with the name of whisky – which can be sold in competition with Scotch.

At one time the companies which shipped malt whisky in bulk put forward an ingenious argument in its defence. They claimed that in the long term admixtures of malt whisky and local spirit would benefit Scotch Whisky as a whole. Admixtures would introduce people who could not afford the genuine article to the flavour of Scotch and, as the standards of living in their countries rose, they would start buying genuine Scotch, and gradually admixtures would disappear from the market.

One can only observe that these forecasts have not been correct. The amount of malt whisky exported in bulk from Scotland fluctuates to some extent from year to year, but trade figures show that the amount now being shipped is roughly the same as that exported fifteen years ago. Another argument sometimes put forward in defence of bulk malt exports is that in volume they are relatively small, accounting for rather less than ten per cent of all the whisky exported from Scotland each year. This is true, but it may be worth pointing out that the malt whisky will be 'blended' with locally distilled spirit. Using perhaps no more than ten or fifteen per cent of Scotch malt in their blends, admixers will be able to produce a whisky that can be passed off as Scotch. One does not need to be a mathematician to realise what this means. The amount of admixed whiskies being produced in the world today may well be not far short of the total global exports of Scotch Whisky.

From time to time the shipping of bulk malt whisky has caused sufficient concern for demands to be made that it should be stopped. MPs, trade union officials and the media have urged the government to ban it. Successive governments, whatever their political complexion, have always found reasons for declining to take any action. Meanwhile, the painting of the Forth Bridge and the frighteningly expensive work of protecting the reputation of Scotch Whisky continue.

Returning to the Raffles Hotel one evening during a short visit to Singapore, I found a note waiting for me from John Reardon. John, at that time the Export Director of Long John Distillers, had found out that I was in Singapore and suggested that we should meet for a drink. To learn that he was in Singapore did not surprise me. In almost any city in the world one is liable to run into an export director or manager from a Scotch Whisky company on a sales trip. That is how the international sales of Scotch have been built.

The following evening we had a glass of Long John in the bar of the Raffles. The hotel with its punkas and mosquito nets and houseboys was pure British Raj. I almost felt that I could feel the ghost of Somerset Maugham waiting for the colonial administrators and their memsahibs to arrive in rickshaws, so that he could listen to them gossiping over their Singapore Slings on the veranda and gather material for another short story of exquisite cynicism.

John and I agreed to go out and have a Chinese meal. He took me to a street in which there seemed to be nothing but Chinese restaurants. People were eating at tables set on the street outside, but at the restaurant he chose we were taken inside to a room that had bare tables and chairs and not much else. There a brawny Chinese in dirty white trousers and a singlet, who looked more like a lascar seaman than a waiter, took our order. From time to time he disappeared into the kitchen at the back, and he could have been the cook as well as the waiter. At that time Chinese food was not as popular in Britain as it now is, and although I had eaten Chinese food on a number of occasions, I had never felt obliged to wrestle with chopsticks. Now I had no choice, for there was not a spoon or fork in the place. The waiter did manage to find us a bottle of Scotch, though.

As we were working our way through a selection of different dishes, all of them delicious, I noticed the lascar waiter pouring himself a drink. The bottle from which he poured, and which he kept on a shelf at the back of the room, was a VSOP cognac. He topped the cognac up with what looked like soda-water and took a liberal gulp. Waiting and cooking in that temperature must have created a good thirst.

John may have noticed me watching the man, for he asked, 'Are you surprised to see him drinking cognac? Don't be. The Chinese love their cognac.'

Cognac, he told me, had been for many years a favourite drink of the Chinese, and Singapore and Hong Kong were among the leading export markets for the cognac trade. The reason for this was not entirely clear, but people said the Chinese had been introduced to cognac in the nineteenth century by sailors of the French navy when it was in China supporting France's colonial aspirations in that region. Their longstanding penchant for brandy made it difficult to interest the Chinese in Scotch. When questioned on their preference, they would say that brandy, unlike Scotch, was a 'heaty' drink and for this reason better for one's health. The exact meaning of the term 'heaty' was never explained, perhaps deliberately, but it seems likely that it is only a euphemism for an aphrodisiac.

Only a few days previously the head of one of France's leading family cognac houses had been in Singapore. To mark the occasion, local businessmen had arranged a private dinner party for him at which his company's oldest and most expensive cognac was served. As the Chinese lifted their glasses to drink his health, the Frenchman's pleasure at the compliment they were paying him quickly evaporated when he saw that to a man they had topped up his priceless cognac with ginger ale.

By the time John had finished this and other stories about Singapore, it was growing late. He had finished eating, but I was pressing on, determined to master the chopsticks.

He looked at me gravely. 'What time did you say your plane for Tokyo leaves tomorrow?'

189

*

On arriving in a foreign city, one of the first things anyone in the whisky business usually does is to tour the shops. He will not be looking for souvenirs to buy but to see what prices are being charged for different categories of Scotch and what brands are on display.

My visit to Tokyo coincided with one of the nation's gift-giving seasons. There are two such seasons: O-Chugen in the middle of the year and O-Seibo at the end. Presents are only given upwards: in other words, a man will be obliged to send a gift to his boss, his landlord, his doctor and his son's schoolteacher. He will not give gifts to those who work under him. The quality and price of the gift to be given is a matter of protocol, to disregard which would mean enormous loss of face. Gifts are also judged by the paper in which they are wrapped, and those most valued will come in the paper of one of Tokyo's three leading departmental stores.

I visited one of these stores soon after reaching Tokyo and found a whole department devoted to a display of gifts. A man would study the display, choose his gifts and pay for them, and the store would send them to the recipient. Alternatively, if he were senior enough, he might send his secretary to the store armed with the visiting cards of the people to whom the gifts would be sent, and on the cards would be marked the price to be paid in each case. Gifts are invariably priced in multiples of 5,000 yen (equivalent to about £20), that being the lowest acceptable sum that one can spend.

Although in comparison with other western and developed countries Japan is a nation of modest drinkers, alcoholic drinks took up a large part of the gift display in the store which I visited. Whisky, brandy and wine carry considerable prestige with the Japanese, particularly among managers and executives. Gifts of Scotch on display ranged from a single

190

bottle of a standard blend to three bottles of a de luxe blend or of a single malt, all beautifully packaged. Since to give a gift priced at even a fraction lower than a multiple of 5,000 yen is taboo, in some cases a gift of a bottle of whisky would be made up to the right figure with the addition of a bar of soap or two tins of soup.

As one would expect, some of the gifts were very expensive. The ultimate in lavishness that I saw was three bottles each of Johnnie Walker Black Label and Chivas Regal priced at so many thousands of yen that, not having a calculator, I could not work it out in bawbees. Even this, I am told, was dwarfed by a whisky marketed specially by James Buchanan and Company in 1986. This was the year when the Emperor of Japan had ruled for sixty years and Queen Elizabeth reached her sixtieth birthday. The whisky was a sixty-year-old single malt from Royal Brackla distillery and it was priced at 600,000 yen, equivalent approximately at that time to £2,800 a bottle. The whole consignment was quickly sold.

On my way back to my hotel from the store, I passed a shop selling wines and spirits. That week it had a special promotion of wine, and one of its windows was completely devoted to one brand of wine, a Château something-or-other. The label on the bottle was decorated with a drawing of what might have been a château in Bordeaux and printed diagonally across it in red letters were the words *'Mise en bouteilles dans nos caves'*. The price seemed attractively low for a French wine, and it was only after asking in the shop that I discovered it was not French but Japanese.

Among the gifts displayed in the department store had been bottles of Japanese whisky, some marked with prices not so much lower than those being asked for bottles of Scotch. The Japanese wine I had seen earlier that day was obviously being 'passed off' to consumers as French wine. So what about the Japanese whisky? At one time Japan had the reputation of being a nation of imitators. Disregarding patent laws or commercial ethics, the Japanese would find ways of producing good copies of Western products and inventions. Later people realised that the Japanese were more than mere mimics. The automobiles, cameras and television sets they were producing were better than those produced in the West and because they had developed a production technology in advance of that used elsewhere, their products were competitive in price.

It was in the 1920s that the Japanese began taking an interest in Scotch Whisky. Not surprisingly their interest was directed at Scotch, the only international whisky in those days, rather than American or Canadian whiskey. Their study of Scotch followed a familiar pattern. Teams were sent to Scotland to visit, photograph and measure distilleries and distillery equipment. Scottish distillers were recruited to advise on the construction and commissioning of distilleries in Japan and on all aspects of distilling, maturation and blending. At first even peat was imported from Scotland, until the Japanese discovered that the peat in their country, although different in chemical composition from Scottish peat, could be used for malting cereals.

Today there are a handful of distilleries in Japan, some of them extremely large. The Japanese claim to be making several different whiskies at each distillery, a claim which not many distillers in Scotland would take seriously. In recent years wine writers have been complimentary about Japanese whiskies, which may simply be part of the 'Let's be nice to the Japanese' cult. On the other hand it is always possible that they are being sponsored by Japanese whisky companies. They write glowingly about the picturesque location and industrial efficiency of Japanese distilleries and of what

Japanese whisky companies are doing for the community and for the arts. One even went so far as to declare that whisky is a 'Japanese heritage'! At the same time, they are surprisingly reticent about how Japanese whisky is made.

Information about the composition of Japanese whisky is hard to unearth. It is usually agreed that there are different grades of Japanese whisky. Analysis carried out in Scotland suggests the whiskies in the lowest and cheapest grades would not qualify for the description of whisky in most countries. It has been suggested that they might be made from molasses imported from India. The higher grades, which are the ones that compete with Scotch Whisky in the Japanese market, appear to contain between fifteen and twenty per cent of Scotch malt whisky, exported to Japan in bulk.

Japan is easily the largest importer of bulk malt whisky, taking over half of the total amount shipped each year from Scotland. The Japanese are a chauvinistic people who believe that their products are superior to those produced anywhere else. For this reason they are reluctant to admit that Scotch malt whisky is an essential component of their best whiskies, since this would be an admission that they are unable to distil malt whisky of a comparable flavour and quality.

Japan is a good market for Scotch Whisky blended and bottled in Scotland, the fourth largest of all export markets. On the latest available figures, sales of Scotch blends in Japan are equivalent to about 27 million bottles. That sounds like a lot of whisky, but it is only about ten per cent of all the whisky drunk by the Japanese. The other ninety per cent is virtually all Japanese blended whisky. Now the volume of Scotch malt whisky being shipped to Japan is greater than the shipments of blended whisky. Were it to be bottled in Japan as single malts, it would be equivalent to about 36 million bottles. But we know it is not being bottled as single malts, but blended with Japanese whisky. If the Japanese are using twenty per cent Scotch malt and eighty per cent Japanese whisky in their blends, this would mean that they are producing about 180 million bottles of blended whisky with a base of Scotch malt to be sold in competition with imported Scotch.

In Scotland, Japanese whisky is not considered a serious threat to Scotch, and most people discount the possibility that it could ever achieve the same international dominance in its field as have cars and cameras. Scots point out that virtually nobody outside Japan drinks Japanese whisky. Its exports are tiny, equal to only some two or three per cent of total sales. The comparable figure for Scotch is almost eighty-five per cent. The Japanese have tried and so far failed to achieve any penetration of the whisky market in the United States, and the most successful Japanese drink there is Midori, a melon-based liqueur, which is nearer to what Scots perceive as typical of Japanese culture.

One cannot help wondering whether this complacency is ill advised. World sales of Scotch reached their peak as long ago as 1978. Since then they have declined, not dramatically, but the trend is unmistakably downward. Realistically one could not have expected the world's thirst for Scotch Whisky to have continued growing indefinitely. The golden years could not continue every year to grow more golden. Is it impossible that as the shadow of Scotch lengthens, we may see the sun of Japan rising in the East?

8

A Question of Taste

A hotel in the West End of London decided that it would open a Scotch Whisky bar. This was to carry a large selection of Scotches, single malts as well as blends, and would be decorated in a Scottish theme, with tartan carpet and curtains and claymores, targes and other reminders of Scotland's valour around the walls. On the day of the official opening two Scotsmen arrived in the bar. Both were wearing the kilt and gave the impression that they might have come straight off the plane from Glasgow.

They both ordered Scotch, choosing their brands and saying that they would take it with lemonade. When they came to pay they were appalled, not by the price of the whisky but by what they were being charged for a tiny bottle of lemonade.

'What is it made of?' one of them asked indignantly. 'Gold dust?'

Any Scot would understand their indignation. Not so long ago in every pub in Scotland a bottle of lemonade would be standing on the bar counter, and whisky drinkers could use it to top up their drams without any charge being made. This story should be compulsory reading for all those *soi-disant* whisky experts who pontificate on how Scotch should be drunk. Mostly they insist that there are only two ways, either undiluted or with a little plain water. If they believe whisky should be drunk neat and they fancy themselves as humorists, they will probably add that there are two things which every good Scot likes naked, and one is his whisky. They, and whoever invented that motheaten old tale, are presumably not aware that every Scotch they drink, single malts as well as blends – will already have been diluted, when water was added to reduce it to 'bottling strength'.

Many Scots take lemonade with their whisky, and why not? There is in fact only one way to drink whisky and that is the way you choose to. Having made that statement, I must revise it and make it clear that Scotch can be drunk in many different ways to suit the occasion, the time of day and the drinker's mood.

In a hotel bar in Dallas I once watched a middle-aged Scot, unmistakable because of his accent, trying to insist on having his Scotch served the way he wanted it. He sent it back once when the glass arrived full of ice-cubes and then a second time because he had seen the barman simply take the ice out with a spoon. As every Scot knows, when that is done you lose a lot of whisky. He wanted the Scotch without ice and with plain water; but no, the pretty waitress was not to add the water, for she might drown the Scotch. So she brought him one glass with the Scotch in it and a glass of plain water and when he tried to pour the water from one glass to the other, he spilt it over the table and his trousers.

People who drink Scotch in foreign countries would do well to consider whether it might not be wisest to drink it the way the natives do. Might there not be a good scientific reason why Americans like their Scotch on the rocks, something to do with the climate, the humidity, body temperature and metabolism? There must be some reason beyond sheer cussedness why Americans take practically every drink on the rocks, even Harvey's Bristol Cream sherry and that Anglo-Irish low alcohol milk shake, Bailey's Irish Cream?

The same could be true of tropical regions. It may be that expatriate Scots have realised instinctively that the 'chota peg' of Scotch they take for their 'sundowner' needs to be more heavily diluted than at home, and the lack of any good, safe water will incline them to soda water.

Most people in the whisky trade and most dedicated Scotch drinkers do prefer to take their dram with an equal amount of pure cool water. This is because, as every whisky blender knows, water releases the aroma of the whisky and allows one to savour its flavour and character. The water must be cool, for nothing can spoil a Scotch more than tepid water taken from a jug that has been standing on the bar for an hour or more. Tap water that is heavily chlorinated should also be avoided, and some of the excellent bottled waters from the Highlands are in any case far better than most tap water.

Although drinking Scotch with a little water or undiluted is undoubtedly the best way to enjoy its true flavour, to be dogmatic about it would be mistaken. Leaving lemonade aside, there are a number of mixed drinks made with Scotch which have always been appreciated and accepted in the Scottish social scene. That does not mean cocktails. Adding blue curacao, peach brandy and coconut to whisky may produce an extravaganza of colour to outdo pop art, but they do nothing for Scotch. A Whisky Mac, on the other hand – Scotch with green ginger wine, Crabbie's, if you can get it – is old enough to be an institution in Scotland. For any golfer coming in off the links in winter with frozen hands there can be no more welcome drink.

In the Caledonian Club, a London haven for exiled Scots, to order one of the most popular after-lunch drinks one simply asks for a Chairman's Special. It is an uncomplicated drink, Scotch malt whisky and the whisky-based liqueur Drambuie, the secret recipe for which, so the Mackinnon family claim, was given to one of their ancestors by Prince Charles Edward and has been kept by them ever since. It is not a story that one should take too lightly, for the Mackinnons of Skye did help Prince Charles when he was a fugitive on the island. This combination of whisky and Drambuie is sometimes also known as a Rusty Nail. No one has ever been able to give a satisfactory explanation for the origin of this name. Could it be because the drink might be the one rusty nail in the coffin-lid, enabling an otherwise doomed over-indulger to make a last-minute escape?

Both the Whisky Mac and the Special, as well as malt whisky on its own, are popular drinks among curlers. Curling is the winter sport of farmers and distillers in Scotland. Once a primitive and largely improvised game, a form of bowls played with granite 'stones' on any convenient stretch of ice, it is now highly organised and competitive. National and international competitions are held, 'bonspiels' as they are called by the curling fraternity, in Europe, Canada and the

United States with prizes worth several thousand dollars.

The most celebrated and one of the oldest bonspiels is the Grand match between two teams of curlers, one from the north of Scotland and one from the south. What makes the match unique is that it may be contested only once, or possibly twice, in any curler's lifetime. At the beginning of each winter the Royal Caledonian Curling Club, the ruling body of the sport in Scotland, nominates the two teams, each made up of three hundred or more 'rinks' of four players. Each rink will be told the name of the rink against which it will curl and also that the match, if it takes place at all, will be played on one of three nominated lochs. It will only take place if at any time during the winter one of the three lochs freezes hard enough to support the weight of the match. That means the weight of the curlers, their curling stones, the other equipment and of course the weight of the many supporters who turn out to watch.

If in the course of the winter it seems likely that one of the three lochs will freeze to the depth required, the curlers are alerted about three days in advance. When the decision to play is finally taken, announcements are made on the eve of the chosen date on radio and television, and early next morning curlers from all over Scotland set out for the loch. John Grant of Glenfarclas who, together with his father, played in the last Grand Match, held in 1979, has described the occasion and showed me a photograph taken on the day. The ice had been marked out and some 2,400 curlers, all wearing something tartan, had assembled when the Lord Elgin, President of the Royal Caledonian Curling Club, arrived by helicopter at eleven o'clock and fired a cannon as a signal to start the match.

The directors of William Teachers had generously brought with them a hogshead of whisky, holding more than a hundred gallons. This may sound as if the match were to become an orgy, but a hundred gallons is only the equivalent of six hundred bottles or a quarter of a bottle for each curler, roughly four large whiskies over a long, cold and strenuous day. The hogshead was positioned on the edge of the loch and by the end of the afternoon it was in danger of falling through the ice, which was melting all around it because of the passage of hundreds of pairs of feet as the curlers came to draw a dram from it.

Another traditional drink associated in Scotland with winter is the Whisky Toddy; a combination of Scotch, Lemon juice and honey, with perhaps a stick of cinnamon. They say it should always be drunk out of a silver mug and never a glass. My silver christening mug, a gift from my godfather, has long ago disappeared into the limbo of a disorganised household and the only silver drinking vessel I possess is a pint tankard, won at golf. I have never had the courage to drink a whisky, however diluted, out of a pint mug but maybe I have been wrong. My friend Michael Martin, formerly of Crabbie's, an expert in these matters, has given me the ultimate cure for a winter chill. Go straight to bed, he says, hang a hat on a peg where you can watch it and keep drinking toddies until you see two hats. I have the golfing tankard ready polished and the whisky, and now all I need is the chill.

Two other Scottish drinks made with whisky are Het Pint and Atholl Brose. Het Pint is a combination of Scotch, mild ale, beaten eggs and nutmeg. It should be served straight out of kettles on Hogmanay and may account for the foul music to be heard on those TV programmes which come out of Glasgow when the celebrations are at their height!

Atholl Brose on the other hand has an aristocratic pedigree, for it is named after the Duke of Atholl. In 1745 he captured his great enemy, the Earl of Ross, by pouring his brose into a well from which the Earl drew water. While the Earl was sleeping off the effects of the brose he was easily seized and made prisoner. The tale, one would have thought, is a dubious recommendation for the drink, which is made from whisky, honey and oatmeal. Mix the oatmeal with water, allow the mixture to stand for forty-five minutes and then pass it through a fine strainer. The resulting liquid should be sweetened with honey and the whisky added, before it is bottled and left to stand for two days before serving.

Even in Scotland there are eccentric souls who experiment with combinations of drinks which might at first appear to be wildly incompatible. Take a Purple Heather – Scotch and créme de cassis – for example. Surely, one would think, that is stretching the Auld Alliance too far. But, improbable though it may seem, with plenty of ice and topped up with soda, a Purple Heather is a good, refreshing, summer drink.

I shall mention only one more example of this type of bartender's brinkmanship and that for two reasons. The first is that I was introduced to it by James Bruxner of Justerini and Brooks, who also introduced me to Californian wines which I discovered are really quite drinkable. The drink, which James called a Bloody Joseph, is in fact a Blood Mary made with Scotch instead of vodka and tabasco sauce instead of Lea and Perrins. I was inclinced to suspect that he was playing a joke on me, but after getting over the initial shock, I decided that the Bloody Joseph had a good deal more depth of flavour and character than a Bloody Mary.

My second reason for mentioning it is sheer vanity. In Rome one day I was taken by a friend to a bar in Via Veneto. The barman asked me what I wished to drink and on an impulse, as inexplicable as it was uncharacteristic, I decided

201

to try one of James Bruxner's Bloody Josephs, but with a flash of inspiration I gave it a new name. A Bannockburn would be much more appropriate, I felt, in memory of Scotland's victory over the English, with the tomato juice and Scotch symbolic of English blood and Scottish spirit. The barman, intrigued, insisted on my writing the recipe for the Bannockburn in a cocktail book which he kept in the bar. Since that time I have seen the recipe included in a number of magazine articles on cocktails. I doubt whether that has made any difference to the sales of Scotch, but perhaps it has helped in a small way to perpetuate the memory of Scotland's greatest victory over her traditional enemy.

When choosing how to take his Scotch, a whisky drinker need only follow his palate and his mood. When deciding which Scotch to choose, a little basic knowledge can be helpful. What information will drinkers find on the label of a bottle of Scotch? The answer is, very little. The description Scotch Whisky will tell them that it has been distilled in Scotland in accordance with the legal definition of Scotch. They can be assured that it will have been matured in oak casks for a minimum of three years. If an age is stated on the label that will be the age of the youngest whisky in the bottle, whether it be a blend or a single malt or single grain whisky. Expressions like 'old,' 'aged', 'selected', 'reserve', 'premium' or 'de luxe' give no guarantees of either age or quality, as they have no legal or regulatory backing.

Blended Scotches fall into three main categories: secondary brands, sometimes derisively called 'cheapies', standard brands and de luxe or premium brands. As a general rule, blended whiskies that are described as premium or de luxe will consist of older whiskies and probably, although companies are reluctant to admit this, they will contain a higher proportion of malt whiskies and a smaller proportion of grain whisky. In the last few years more companies are marketing their de luxe blends with an age shown on the label and usually this will be twelve years.

The number of blended Scotch Whiskies that are on sale in the United Kingdom and the two hundred countries to which Scotch is exported is incalculable. Hundreds, even thousands, of trademarks or names are registered, but this means little. Brand owners may decide to register names that are similar to that of their brand, simply as a form of protection. For linguistic or translation reasons it might be expedient to sell a blended whisky under a different name in some export markets. Finally there are the scores of 'own label' brands, the vast majority of which the ordinary consumer will never see. So in reality the choice of a blended Scotch to buy or drink is much narrower than one might imagine.

The choice is even more restricted in pubs, particularly pubs in England where, because of distribution arrangements and 'deals', the selection of brands of Scotch is usually miserly. Most pubs will have at the most two 'pouring' Scotches on the optics and if one is lucky two or three more in an inconspicuous place on the shelves below.

When buying a bottle of Scotch in an off-licence, how should one make one's choice? Price is not always a guide to quality, but as a general rule the better blends of Scotch will be more expensive because they cost more to produce. 'Special offers' can be tempting, but one has a right to ask why it is that a whisky company needs to unload its brands on the market in this way. We all have friends who after pouring us a whisky in their homes will ask, 'What do you think of this Glen Scurvy? I picked it up at Whizzo Supermarkets. It's their own whisky. Of course, I know nothing about Scotch, but it does seem to me as good as anything I've ever tasted.' What he is really saying is that there was no way he was going to pay another £2 for a bottle of The Famous Grouse. Supermarkets are in the business of making money, not whisky, and their first requirement to the whisky company which blends and bottles their whisky for them is that it must meet the price they are prepared to pay.

Another way of selling Scotch more cheaply at the expense of the consumer is by bottling it at lower strengths. Fortunately this practice will soon come to an end for, after years of campaigning, the Scotch Whisky Association has been able to obtain a legal definition of Scotch which stipulates a minimum strength. Some low-strength Scotches will still be found in the market but they will gradually disappear. The label on a bottle of Scotch should tell you that it contains at least forty per cent alcohol by volume. For some Scotches bought abroad and in duty-free shops the figure will probably be forty-three per cent.

One often hears people, especially patriotic Scotsmen, say that there is no such thing as a bad Scotch Whisky. Loyalty compels me to agree with this as a general maxim, but I do know of whisky firms who seem to be going to some lengths to refute it.

If price is one guide to quality, another and more important one is reputation. The reputation of the leading brands of Scotch Whisky have not been built up overnight by clever advertising and marketing. Attempts have been made to launch new brands of Scotch with massive advertising campaigns and all the hyperbole that Madison Avenue can invent, but without exception they have failed. The sales of leading brands of Scotch have been built up over years by the Walkers and the Dewars and the Gloags and the Teachers. Their reputations would not have endured unless they were based on quality and consistency. Anyone wishing to buy

Scotch to keep at home and offer to his friends would be wise to make his choice from these and the other 'flagship' brands.

A golf writer, Bernard Darwin I suspect it was, once remarked that a man can be virtuous, God-fearing, a good husband and devoted father and still miss a two-foot putt. In the same way I accept that a whisky blender can be a fine, honest fellow, skilled in his craft and dedicated to it and yet he still may be unable to produce a blend of Scotch that I would wish to have as my favourite and drink regularly. Any whisky drinker may well find out that he feels the same way.

Experiment is the only way to discover which blended Scotches suit your taste and which you will tolerate when your favourite brand is not available. As a general rule standard brands are best for day to day drinking and twelve-year-old blends kept for the occasions when you have the time to enjoy them and the right company with which to share your enjoyment.

Secondary brands are best kept for exotic cocktails, if you must make them, or for cooking. David Blair, the Walker Cup golfer and at one time head of James Buchanan and Company, would turn up his nose in scorn when people suggested that the company should promote recipes using Scotch. 'I don't want Black and White to be thought of as a cooking whisky,' he would say, believing that it would place the brand on the same level as the cheap sherry which cooks use.

Even people connected with the whisky business sometimes find strange uses for whisky. David Simpson, a director of White Horse Distillers, used to work tirelessly for his brand and for Scotch Whisky generally and was always ready to parade at receptions, whisky tastings and press conferences. His wife Celia, a wonderfully laid-back, good-natured woman, did not mind his frequent absences from home, but from time to time complained that David would never take her with him to these functions.

Once he did take her. The occasion was a reception for a party of French journalists who had been on a tour of distilleries. Hearing that the journalists were all men and that there would be few ladies among the hosts, he also took his very pretty daughter Shirley, who was good at parties and who spoke French. During the course of the evening one journalist, seeing Celia Simpson with a glass of Campari in her hand, asked her if she never drank Scotch.

Shirley, who was standing nearby and saw her mother struggling with French, decided to be helpful. 'No, Mummy never drinks Scotch,' she said, 'but she finds it very useful for removing stains from carpets.'

In due course the story appeared in *Le Monde* or *Figaro* or some other Paris newspaper. David's French agent sent him a copy. A few days later he telephoned him to commiserate.

'Don't worry,' he said, 'it could happen to anyone.'

'Worry? I'm delighted!' David replied. 'I'm keeping the clipping in my wallet and every time Celia asks me why I don't take her to business functions, I'll take it out and show it to her!'

Choosing a blended Scotch may seem no more than a prosaic scanning of a few bottles in a bar or on a wine merchant's shelves, but when one turns to single malts one is immediately in an Aladin's cave of dazzling options. And yet, as in all caves of treasure, all that glisters is not gold.

The Pot Still pub in Glasgow has one of the largest selections of single malt Scotches that I have seen. Ranged along its shelves one can see more than three hundred bottles, some bearing names which everyone knows – Glenfiddich, Glenmorangie, Glenfarclas, Cardhu – others of which many whisky drinkers may never have heard – Ardbeg, Glenburgie, Littlemill. In the selection one can see the same whiskies bottled at different ages, five, eight, twelve, fifteen, twenty-one years old. What may be even more confusing is that the same single malt will appear with two or even three different styles of label. This is not confined to The Pot Still, and one will find the same in many shops and pubs.

A single malt Scotch Whisky is by definition the whisky of one distillery. Since there are only a hundred and three malt whisky distilleries in Scotland, the array of bottles in The Pot Still can only confuse anyone who is new to the whisky scene. Part of that confusion may be dispelled if the existence of the different labels is explained.

For many years distilleries, in addition to laying down stocks of their malt whisky to bottle when it is mature, have 'filled' casks not only for the blending companies but for whisky merchants. The whisky merchants may have used the whisky to produce their own blends or they may have bottled it as single malts, using the name of the distillery but their own labels. Until recently the number of single malts put on sale by these 'independent bottlers' was relatively small and the volume of their sales insignificant. With the rapidly growing public interest in Scotch malt whisky the picture has changed. Independent bottlers like Gordon and Macphail of Elgin and Cadenhead's Whisky Shop of Edinburgh are now putting on the market a wide range of single malts, many at different ages, a large proportion of which are not bottled for sale by the distilleries themselves.

This development has not been welcomed by everybody and some distillers are particularly unhappy about it. Their argument goes something like this. The name of a distillery – let us use an imaginary one 'Loch Maree', as an example – is in effect a trademark. Not only are the owners of the distillery entitled to benefit from the sale of whisky under that trade-mark, but it is their responsibility to ensure that the whisky is matured and bottled in a style and to a quality which will enhance its reputation. They cannot have any control over the quality of a Loch Maree single malt whisky put out by an independent bottler. If a whisky drinker buys a bottle of Loch Maree which is below standard in any respect, then it is the name of the whisky that will suffer, not that of the bottler.

The counter to this argument is that the independent bottlers have bought the whisky in good faith and are entitled to bottle and sell it as a single malt whisky from Loch Maree, for that is what it is. One has to concede that independent bottlers have made available to consumers a large number of single malts, which they would otherwise not have been able to buy and taste. On recent visits to The Pot Still and to two well-known whisky shops, Lamberts in Edinburgh and the Soho Wine market in London, I counted more than twenty-five single malts which are not currently being bottled for sale by the owners of the distilleries.

This widening of choice to the consumer sounds fine in principle, but people who know their Scotch would, if they were honest, agree that many of these malts, although more than acceptable in a blend, are not worth drinking as single malts. The judgment of whisky blenders who place single malt whiskies in classifications according to quality would be the most reliable guide, and I am sure that they must be surprised to find that some of the whiskies in the lower classifications are being bottled for sale.

This does not mean that these whiskies are undrinkable, but merely that in the view of experts they do not have the character, the flavour and the quality to be expected in a good single malt Scotch. There are malt whisky distilleries in Scotland which distil in, shall we say, unconventional ways. I once visited one where they claimed that by adjusting the heads of the stills they were able to produce different whiskies. One would think that if a distillery could produce a malt whisky good enough to be in demand among either blenders or whisky drinkers, it would not need to manipulate its stills to make another.

The bottling of single malts has become a controversial subject. In essence the argument is not one about consumer choice but about money. Preferring like all cowards to remain neutral, the only advice I would offer to a newcomer to malt whisky is that when he has a choice, he should pick the single malt that has been bottled by the owners of the distillery. In that way he can know that he will be drinking a malt whisky of the style, age and quality which the distiller believes to be the best for his whisky. Moreover, whiskies bottled by the distiller are more likely to be consistent, as an independent bottler will usually have only limited stocks of mature whisky at his disposal.

This means examining the label. One wishes that, as for French wine, there might be a simple phrase on every label to show where and by whom it has been bottled. 'Château bottled' would clearly not be appropriate, but perhaps a phrase equivalent to '*Mise en bouteilles par le propriétaire*' might suffice. Like many sensible ideas which would help remove some of the confusion caused by the proliferation of labels and the number of single malts, it is probably now too late to introduce such a scheme.

If the name of the bottler is one factor to guide a choice of a malt whisky, a second and more important one is its age. A bottled single malt whisky will probably contain whisky that has been matured in several different casks. If an age is stated on the label of the bottle, then it must be that of the youngest whisky that has been used. Averaging is not allowed.

What should one say about the right age for a malt whisky? Only that there is no such thing. One must not be dogmatic, but few malt whiskies are sold at under seven years and if you were to regard this as a minimum, you would at least be sure of drinking a whisky that is mature. As another general rule, malt whiskies with a fuller flavour, such as those from Speyside and from the islands, need longer to reach their best. Lowland malts and those which are relatively mild in flavour probably do not need to mature for longer than ten years and may not improve after that time.

There is not, nor can there ever be, a maximum age for a single malt whisky. A number are now available at fifteen years and a few at eighteen, twenty-one and even twenty-five. Whisky can continue to improve beyond fifteen years. At one distillery I was once given a glass of malt whisky that had been distilled more than thirty-five years previously. They told me that it had not been kept for all those years deliberately, but simply because the records of a particular batch of whisky distilled for private customers had been accidentally destroyed and they did not know to whom the whisky belonged. In many respects it was a fine whisky, very sweet and mellow, not unlike armagnac, but in the background one could detect a strong flavour of wood.

Scotch Whisky does extract some of its flavour from the wood of the cask in which it matures. That is an essential part of the process of maturation. However, when one can begin to taste the wood itself, that surely is a sign that the whisky has been left in the cask too long. In any event, when I drink malt whisky I have no wish to taste armagnac. Why should one be fobbed off with a poor relation of cognac instead of the noblest spirit of them all, malt whisky?

As a general rule between ten and fifteen years is a good age for a single malt Scotch, ten for the Lowland and the less

210

full-flavoured Highland malts, twelve or fifteen for the island and the best of the Speyside malts. This is not to say that one cannot find some splendid eighteen or twenty-one or even twenty-five-year-old malts, but it is likely that if they are better than the same whisky at fifteen years, it will only be marginally so. In many cases the flavour of sherry or of wood will dominate, concealing the subtle complexities of the whisky. Knowledgeable whisky drinkers will probably feel that they are not worth the extra price which will be charged for them.

Some years before malt whisky became fashionable, a tasting of single malts was held for leading wine writers in London's Charing Cross Hotel. To call it a tasting is misleading. It was primarily an educational exercise, intended to introduce malt whisky to the country's leading wine writers, many of whom appeared at that time not to have even heard of it. Michael Martin of John Crabbie and Company gave a talk, explaining how malt whisky is made and the difference between single malts and blended whisky. To illustrate his talk a large number of samples of different single malts were circulated among the audience.

After the talk the wine writers took part in a contest. The test they were given was not complicated. Samples of a dozen single malts, all of which the audience had been able to nose during the talk, had been poured into numbered glasses. Each contestant was given a list of the malts and the test was to identify and name the malts, either by nosing them as a blender would or, if they wished, by tasting them.

Any whisky blender would have been able to pick out the different samples without much difficulty, for they included several malts which fall into the category of 'once nosed never forgotten'. Laphroaig was one and Glenmorangie another. People with little experience would obviously find the test more difficult, but one would have thought that wine writers, who are used to nosing and tasting different wines, might have an advantage. In the event the winner of the contest, for which the prize was a bottle of fifteen-year-old Glenlivet, had a score of five correct answers out of twelve. A mathematician friend tells me that this is only a fraction better than the average score one might expect to get simply by guessing. In spite of this disappointing result, the wine writers appeared to have enjoyed the occasion and most of them wrote articles on malt whisky not long afterwards. Some even went to Scotland and toured the distilleries.

What interested me was the expressions they used when writing about the whiskies they had tasted. In the main they fell back on a bastardised version of wine writers' language, pretentious and coy and very largely meaningless. To para-phrase the Duke of Wellington's remark about kilted High-landers, I don't know what they did to their readers, but by God they confused me. The other day a wine columnist of a Sunday newspaper, reviewing the wines available in a super-market, offered some gems. 'A crispy, cream-cheese scent and lemon-rind acidity' was one. 'Warm, sensuous and approachable, with spicy plum and liquorice flavour and chewy tannins' was another. One could not help wondering whether the author had lost his way in the supermarket and had been nosing among the grocery shelves.

Now much the same kind of flowery, esoteric language is being used by those who write about malt whisky. From the pages of the many books on Scotch that have been published one can compile a litany of curious nouns and adjectives used to describe the flavour of different single malt whiskies: marzipan, linseed, bitter chocolate, peppermint, flowering currants, orangey, buttery and the evocative 'wet grass on a rainy day'. They say much for the inventive imagination of the authors, but one doubts whether after reading them the whisky lover is any wiser.

Using one flavour to describe another is a risky gambit, very likely to mislead. The customer who buys a bottle of a recommended single malt and expects to taste his favourite linseed may well feel aggrieved when all he can savour is wet grass on a rainy day.

Recently I was shown a 'malt whisky wheel' devised by a whisky company, the purpose of which is apparently to help whisky drinkers to identify the single malts to be found in Scotland. I would have dismissed it as a practical joke or a marketing gimmick had I not seen a very similar 'flavour wheel' produced by one of the whisky industry's research establishments. Both consist of a number of concentric circles, and each circle offers a number of phrases to describe the flavour of a whisky. The phrases in the first circle are mainly technical and would mean something to a distiller, but as one moves outward from the hub of both wheels the selection of adjectives and expressions is disconcerting. 'Sweaty', 'Kippery', 'Burnt tyres', 'Blotting paper' 'Rancid' and 'Cabbage water' are not analogies which ever spring to my mind when nosing a malt whisky. There are no kippers to be found in Lock Maree and if any friend of mine thought that the whisky reminded him of 'stale fish', I would recommend a visit to a good ear, nose and throat surgeon.

When they discuss the flavour and character of a whisky, distillers and blenders use prosaic terms which can be easily understood. 'Sweet', 'mellow', 'pungent', 'delicate', 'sharp' and 'robust' are simple and unambiguous expressions that are unlikely to cause confusion. Even these, though, are open to different interpretations and responses, for our senses of smell and taste are subjective and highly individual. I have

213

known people shake their heads apologetically and mutter 'fiery' after taking a sip of a fifteen-year-old malt whisky, generally recognised to be among the smoothest and most mellow of all single malts.

These differing perceptions make it difficult to offer advice on the choice of malt whiskies. If one is asked to name the best single malt, one can and should refuse. A whisky one would wish to take with one's coffee after dinner would not be what one might wish to drink when standing up to one's thighs in the water of the Spey. A request to name say the twelve best single malts is more difficult to sidestep. After all, why should one not be willing to name one's favourites? On the other hand, taste is so subjective that listing one's preferences could be misleading and in any case smacks of conceit.

As a way out of this dilemma, I invited a number of friends, all in the whisky business and all dedicated to their work, to give me the names of their favourite malt whiskies. I asked for their personal favourites from the whole spectrum of malts, taking no account of the different classifications, and added a list of the malts which I most enjoy drinking. Then from all the lists I selected the twelve names which appeared most frequently.

There was not as great a degree of consensus as one might expect. Some friends had listed malts which have never excited any great enthusiasm in me and some notable names were missing. To have listed the twelve in order of merit would have been not only complicated but unfair so they are placed in alphabetical order. Against each name is the location of the distillery, two or three words describing its flavour and finally the age at which it should best be drunk. The description and the suggested age are purely my opinion, and it may well be that the distillers of the whiskies will challenge these.

TWELVE OF THE BEST

Balvenie	Dufftown	12
	delicate, slightly sweet, fragrant	
Bruichladdich	Islay	10
	mild for an Islay malt, dry	
Cardhu	Knockando	12
	faintly peaty, full-bodied	
Cragganmore	Ballindalloch	12
	rich, sweetish, malty	
Dalmore	Alness	12
	strong sherry, hint of the sea	
Glenfarclas	Ballindalloch	12–15
	powerful, classic, beautifully rounded	
Glenmorangie	Tain	10
	sweet, fresh	
Highland Park	Orkney	12
	smoky, malty, lingers	
Linkwood	Elgin	12
	dry, subtle, smooth	
Longmorn	Longmorn	15
	fragrant, full-bodied, complex	
Macallan	Craigellachie	12–15
	beautifully rich, full, sherry	
Talisker	Isle of Skye	10
	faintly briny, powerful, warming	

The final decisions on which whiskies should be included and which omitted were extremely close. Three malts in particular – The Glenlivet, Mortlach and Auchentoshan – were unlucky to have 'missed the cut', as they say in golf. Personally, I was surprised to see Bruichladdich in the list. For choice I would not include any Islay malts in my selection of twelve, but if I were obliged to pick one it would be either Lagavulin or Bowmore. As it is, those are my 'Twelve of the Best' and no doubt I will be caned for my impertinence in due course.

The malt whiskies of Scotland are unmatched, not only in the variety of flavours which they offer but in their complexity. Using the latest techniques of gas chromatography and mass spectrometry, research scientists have been able to identify some six hundred constituents in Scotch Whisky. Only ten years ago just three hundred had been identified and new technologies may well result in more constituents being discovered in the years ahead. These congenerics, as they are called, contribute to the flavour of the whisky, but there is no way of knowing how or to what extent. In an effort to relate the chemical composition to its flavour, the industry's research establishments run programmes of sensory evaluation. Panels of specially trained volunteers are asked to nose different samples of whisky and to record their impressions of the flavour and character of each. Clearly such experiments are of some help in discovering how the constituents of a whisky affect its flavour, but any relationship there may be will at best be imprecise and might well be illusory.

Our senses are subjective and personal. No scientist can know whether what you taste in a glass of, let us say, Highland Park malt whisky is identical to the taste I would experience. If only for this reason, no scientist will ever be able to produce a 'tailor-made' Scotch that he knows will produce the same sensory response in every whisky drinker. Most of us would thank the Lord for that.

To find out which single malt whiskies suit one's taste ultimately one needs to drink them; and not just one glass, for a good malt may be slow to reveal the full subtlety of its character. Experimenting, trying out the different Highland, Lowland and island malts can be a slow but delightful voyage of discovery.

9

Crossroads

Valerie Blackie worked for a marketing company that specialised in arranging promotions for companies in the drinks
industry. Her job was to 'sell' the ideas for these promotions,
convincing companies that the promotions would result in
spectacular increases in the sales of their whisky, wine or soft
drinks. Valerie was intelligent, articulate, pretty and what the
Americans call a 'mover and a shaker'. Either her moving or
her shaking or both were vibrant enough to get her an
appointment to see Arthur Webb, at that time Managing
Director of John Walker & Sons in the company's luxurious
London offices in St James's Street. In the normal way she

would have had to make her sales pitch to a member of the company a good deal lower in the pecking order.

Arthur listened politely to what Valerie had to propose. Then with a charming smile he asked, 'Miss Blackie, can you give me a good reason why I should agree to pick up this very costly idea you have put forward? My whisky, Johnnie Walker, is the biggest selling Scotch in the world.'

'Ah, Mr Webb,' Valerie countered, 'but have you ever wondered that it may not always be?'

Her riposte was fairly conventional, one would have thought, standard stuff in any manual of salesmanship, but it had a surprising effect. Arthur, normally urbane and self-confident, stared at Valerie and then closed his eyes for a moment, as though in pain.

'Miss Blackie,' he confided with a totally uncharacteristic frankness. 'That is my recurring nightmare!'

That incident happened some years ago when the world sales of Scotch Whisky were growing rapidly. Johnnie Walker is still the largest selling Scotch, but was Arthur Webb's nightmare an intuition, a touch of clairvoyance, giving him a glimpse into the future not just of his whisky, but of all Scotch Whisky? Within a few years almost every distillery in Scotland was reducing the amount of whisky it made, several of them were 'mothballed', and some closed, never to reopen.

The media and city analysts immediately accused the industry of 'over-production'. Too much whisky had obviously been distilled, but the accusations implied that whisky companies had wantonly and irresponsibly distilled large quantities in the hope that they might be able to sell it. That kind of thinking is based on a naive ignorance of how the whisky business operates. Almost all the malt and grain whisky distilled in any one year in Scotland is made 'to order', as it were, against fillings ordered in advance by whisky-blending companies. Because all Scotch must be allowed to mature, blending companies, when deciding how much whisky to lay down, have to forecast what they are likely to be selling four or five years ahead or, in the case of single malts and de luxe whiskies, as much as fifteen or eighteen years ahead. They must also take into account that some two per cent of that whisky will evaporate every year while it is maturing. This is a problem unique to the whisky business, and it means that the amount of whisky distilled in any one year represents the combined sales forecasts of all the companies who market Scotch Whisky.

For more than thirty years after the Second World War, world sales of Scotch increased steadily at an average growth rate of between eight and nine per cent a year. As long as this growth continued, blenders had to lay down stocks of whisky well in excess of what they were selling at any one time. In general, their sales forecasting was reasonably accurate throughout this period, production keeping pace with the increases in world sales. There was some slowing down in the early 1970s but sales continued to rise until they reached a peak in 1978. Since then there have been bad years, followed by slightly better years, but the sales of 1978 have not yet been achieved again.

With hindsight it is easy to say that the Scotch Whisky trade should have realised that this falling off in demand was imminent and cut back on distillation, but how could it have known? Even now people are not agreed on the reasons for this levelling off in demand. Some blame it on a world recession, but if there was recession, why did not sales continue to grow after it had passed?

Others have suggested that the fall in sales was due to a change in consumer tastes. The largest decline in the demand for Scotch in the 1970s was in the United States, and this decline has continued. We were told that Americans were switching away from 'brown goods', in other words whisky, to 'white goods', meaning gin and vodka. This may well have been true but, if so, why were people switching? Almost certainly it was because they believed, erroneously, that white spirits contain less calories then brown spirits and are therefore less fattening and better for health. Confirmation of this theory can be found in the fact that not long afterwards Americans began switching altogether from spirits, white as well as brown, to wine coolers, spritzers and other low-alcohol drinks. This concern for health, which has since become an unhealthy obsession, was summed up by the US Surgeon-General, C. Everitt Koop, who in 1988 declared that 'one day America will have to choose between alcohol and health. She can't have both.' The anti-alcohol lobby in a country where one-third of the population are total abstainers is always strong, and it has allied itself with the health lobby to campaign against alcohol in any form, calling for higher taxes, a ban on alcohol advertising and other restrictive measures.

Whatever the reason, sales of Scotch in the United States have fallen by some forty per cent over the last ten years. Fortunately for Scotland, this decline in sales has almost entirely been made up by increases elsewhere and by the opening of new markets for Scotch in different parts of the world.

A current advertisement for The Famous Grouse whisky carries the caption 'Quality in an Age of Change'. The copy-writer who composed that phrase may not have fully appreciated the significance of the words he was choosing. The past three decades have been an era of continuing change for Scotch. There have been changes in the way it is produced and changes in the way it is marketed and sold. Equally important, though perhaps less noticeable, there have been

changes in the perception of Scotch among drinkers and in
the consumers' attitude to drinking. Finally, there have been
far-reaching changes in the structure of the whisky industry,
with the gradual disappearance of small independent firms
and the concentration of the production and sales of Scotch in
a few large multi-national drinks companies.

Changes in distilling and blending have been spread over a
number of years. They began with the gradual phasing out of
floor maltings as companies either built large mechanical
maltings or purchased the malt they needed from professional maltsters. Probably no more than half a dozen of the a
hundred and two malt whisky distilleries in Scotland now
have floor maltings, and some of these have only been kept
going as an attraction for the visitors who call and can then
be shown a traditional aspect of distilling.

The coal-firing of pot stills has largely been replaced by
steam heating or oil-firing and in many distilleries stainless
steel is now being used in place of the traditional spruce or
larch to make washbacks. In an increasing number of distilleries one finds automatic or semi-automatic control systems
and panels with diagrams and coloured lights which show
the progress of operations from the discharge of the malt
from malt hoppers through milling, mashing, fermentation
and distillation. Clearly the main object of these changes has
been to reduce the number of people employed in distilleries
and, as a consequence to save labour costs. Most malt whisky
distilleries probably now employ fewer than half the number
of people they did thirty years ago.

The changes that have taken place in the blending of
whisky are less visible. Increasingly whisky companies have
their 'fillings' of mature whisky, malt whisky as well as grain,
brought down from the distilleries to the blending halls in
road tankers. The casks are disgorged into the tankers and

can then be left at the distilleries to be refilled. Until recently it used to be normal practice for a sample to be drawn from every cask, and these samples would be examined by the blender and his team before the whisky was blended and bottled. This can no longer happen if casks are emptied at the distilleries and any sampling must be done there.

One cannot help feeling that the role and the importance of the whisky blender is changing and that it has lost much of its mystique. Some companies make no mention of the blender in their publicity brochures and talk instead of 'quality control'. One reason for these changes must clearly be to reduce the costs of production. This is entirely accept-able, although one might observe that making whisky is hardly labour-intensive. The whole Scotch Whisky industry employs only about sixteen thousand people who between them earn the country some £1.7 billion through exports. Another reason for technical changes is to improve control of the whisky-making processes and therefore the quality and consistency of the whisky. It is at least arguable that sophisti-cated systems of control are not needed in making whisky. A number of distillers have told me that they believe that most whisky distilleries are now 'over engineered' and that the basic simplicity of the processes does not warrant the intro-duction of costly production systems.

Tradition cannot be defended simply as tradition, and the ultimate test of these changes is whether they have resulted in improvements in the quality of Scotch Whisky. This is a question to which there cannot be a finite answer. Quality, like beauty, is in the eye of the beholder or rather in his palate. Moreover, if one is measuring the quality of whisky today against that of the past, one must also rely on memory. And who can remember what one particular brand of whisky tasted like even five years ago?

We are all entitled to our opinions. My own view is that the standard brands of blended Scotch have changed and many of them appear to have lost their individuality. With notable exceptions they seem to have moved much closer to each other in flavour. I find that certain brands for which I did not particularly care are now quite palatable, though not very exciting. Conversely, some old favourites appear to have lost their appeal, lighter in flavour now than they used to be, perhaps because they are being bottled at an earlier age. Over the past few years whisky companies, individually or collectively through the Pentlands Scotch Whisky Research Unit, have invested in research. Research has no doubt brought a better understanding of the composition of whisky and improved methods of controlling the processes of making it. This may in turn have led to a degree of uniformity in the processes. That would not affect the individuality of single malt whiskies, but individuality can easily be 'ironed out' by blending, if the blender so wishes. One could understand that owners of lesser known and less successful brands might wish to alter their blends and model them on the market leaders.

If there has been any decline in the quality of standard brands, another reason for it may be economic. Archie Watson, the chairman of Charles Mackinlay and Company, and in his day the doyen of whisky men, used to say that behind every blend of Scotch there is a conflict, an argument between the blender and the accountant. The blender takes a pride in his blend, on which his reputation depends, and wishes to maintain its quality regardless of expense. The accountant is always looking for ways of reducing costs. He will want to know why that Loch Maree malt whisky, which is part of the company's blend, has to be matured for five years. Could it not be used at four years? Does that extra year make so much difference? Anyway, would the consumer notice the difference? And if the blender finds himself short of Loch Maree, does the company really have to go out and buy more in the broking market? Could they not use another single malt, which they can obtain on a reciprocal exchange basis with another blending company? In the whisky business, as in all industries, the power of the accountant is growing.

My own impression is that a polarisation is developing in the quality of Scotch Whiskies, with standard brands in decline while the quality of single malts and premium Scotches has improved. This is reflected in the presentation and packaging of these whiskies and in the prices that are being charged for them. The regulations on age labelling has helped in this respect. If one is going to the expense of keeping a whisky for twelve years so that one may label it as such, it makes economic sense to make sure that it is of the highest possible quality.

A few days ago I was in Kay's Bar in Jamaica Street, a part of Edinburgh not far from Queen Street Gardens. The pub is unlike most other Edinburgh pubs, which tend to be uninviting places, garish and noisy if they cater for tourists or full of the sombre gloom that serious drinkers are supposed to prefer. Kay's is pleasantly scruffy and has a character of its own, its habitués an interesting assortment: young professional men with pretensions to be yuppies, retired folk from the expensive houses in Herriot Row, who go there in cardigans and while away the mornings doing crossword puzzles and exchanging clues across the bar, working men from a new housing development nearby. The bar also has an excellent range of malt whiskies and offers a 'Malt of the Month' at a discounted price. That day it was Isle of Jura.

I had gone to Kay's to meet Angus, a friend of many years,

who had once worked as an export salesman for an Edinburgh whisky firm but, when the firm had been taken over, had switched successfully to selling insurance. He had kept his contacts and his many friends in the whisky business. I found him in the bar talking to Bruce, a young solicitor. They offered to buy me a dram and I chose Glen Mhor, a whisky which would not be around much longer. Glen Mhor and Glen Albyn were two distilleries in Inverness, once owned by Willie Birnie, a celebrated whisky character, which were both fatal casualties of the whisky slump and were closed and then demolished in the early 1980s.

'Come and join in the wake,' Angus said, lifting his glass to me.

'What wake?'

'A wake for the passing of Scotch Whisky,' Bruce replied.

The cause of their pessimism, it appeared, was a recent television programme on the Scotch Whisky industry. The programme had not itself been especially pessimistic about the future of Scotland's leading industry, but had shown graphically that almost the whole of it was now owned and managed from outside Scotland. It had also reported that on the latest available figures both the export and home sales of Scotch were falling.

I tried to reassure them, paraphrasing the old joke that reports of Scotch Whisky's death had been greatly exaggerated. At first they would not be reassured. Scotch Whisky, Angus pointed out, would be only one of many interests of a multi-national drinks group. If sales of Scotch continued to fall, it would be understandable if the multi-national group were to cut back on its investment in Scotch and concentrate on other drinks, German lager, for example, or Spanish wine. Large companies had to be more concerned with making money than making whisky. Today profits were all important. A company's profits had to keep increasing and preferably at a rate faster than inflation, or its share price would fall, leaving it vulnerable to a take-over bid.

'This obsession with profits,' Bruce said, 'is the reason for all the changes that have been introduced. The whole nature of distilling has been destroyed. It is no longer a craft.'

He told us that he had heard of one distillery which had been so automated that it would soon be run by only two men. 'Think what that will mean for employment in the Highlands. This would never be allowed to happen if Scots were running the industry.' Bruce is an ardent Scottish Nationalist.

We lunched in the back room of the pub, the Library Bar, as they call it. I ordered Arbroath smokies, nervously, afraid that just the mention of the name might provoke Bruce into more nationalist fervour. Arbroath was where the famous Declaration appealing for Scottish independence was signed in 1320. As we ate, we talked about some of the difficulties Scotch Whisky faces today.

'Most of our problems,' Bruce declared, 'are the fault of the government. No English government has ever given a toss for the Scotch Whisky trade. The export of whisky in bulk from Scotland should have never been allowed.'

Although I was inclined to agree with his last statement, I felt I had to defend the record of the government in recent years. Stimulated by vigorous lobbying from the Scotch Whisky Association, the government had used all the pressure of diplomacy to have trade barriers and discriminatory taxes reduced in Far East markets. Even the Prime Minister had intervened personally on the industry's behalf. Similarly, the government had managed to secure agreement for a satisfactory definition of Scotch in the European Community, which was essential for the long-term future of the industry.

I told Angus and Bruce that in my view the most serious threat that the Scotch Whisky trade faced was from the anti-alcohol lobby. The American obsession with health had already begun to cross the Atlantic, and in Britain the medical profession had allied itself with anti-alcohol organisations and was telling us to drink less and less.

'Doctors are saying that?' Bruce asked in disbelief. 'I find that strange. In Scotland, the definition of an alcoholic has always been anyone who drinks more than his doctor.'

'Not long ago,' Angus remarked, 'the British Medical Association was saying that four Scotches a day helped give protection against heart disease.'

What he said was true. There is a mass of evidence that alcohol does give protection against coronary heart disease and that spirits give this protection more than wine or beer. Alcohol is also an excellent tranquilliser, helping to relieve stress and reduce insomnia, particularly among the elderly. Some National Health Service doctors have urged that they should be allowed to prescribe it for their patients.

Knowing that the whisky they were drinking was doing them good seemed to dissipate some of the funereal gloom I had detected in Angus and Bruce when I arrived. I raised their spirits still further by giving them the good news about Scotch. Although demand for Scotch as a whole might have levelled off, the sales of single malt Scotches and de luxe blends were increasing. Industry statistics showed that world sales of single malts had almost trebled in the last five years. People might not be drinking more Scotch, but they were drinking better.

'High time too!' Bruce said. 'Now perhaps people are beginning to realise that malt whisky is the only true Scotch.'

There was no way in which I was going to become entangled in an argument on the merits of blended Scotch

227

and single malts. We had finished our lunch, so I ordered three whiskies for us to drink with our coffee. Angus and Bruce asked for single malts, a Cardhu and a Macallan, but to show my nonalignment I ordered a Chivas Regal de luxe whisky.

We raised our glasses, not as an act of defiance to the medical profession but as a gesture of our faith in the future of Scotch Whisky, which my friend Chester had so aptly described as Scotland's heritage.

After lunch Bruce returned to his offices, which were just round the corner, and Angus and I walked back towards Princes Street.

'Do you know,' I remarked, passing on a piece of information which Bill Bewsher, the Director General of the Scotch Whisky Association had given me only that morning, 'As we are walking here, throughout the world twenty nine bottles of Scotch are being sold every second?'

'That reminds me,' Angus said. 'We're running short of Scotch at home. I'll pop into Lamberts for a second and make it thirty bottles.'

Index

Index

Index